THE JOURNEY OF SAME-SEX SURROGACY

DISCOVERING ULTIMATE JOY

By Jason Warner

ISBN: 061589562X
ISBN 13: 9780615895628
Library of Congress Control Number: 2013954111
Zygote Publishing, Franklin, TN

Book Summary:

Revealing shocking difficulties, life-changing decisions, uncertain territory, and reaching into the depth of his heart and soul, Jason shares an intricate love story that is at once embracing and enlightening, involving the current controversial laws and issues that continue to trouble America and threaten the equality, liberty, and justice for all. This is just one of many untold stories about bringing a child into this magical world and discovering ultimate joy.

Acknowledgements:

There are many people I want to thank and acknowledge. Thank you to deMarco's and my parents. I believe that having great parents gave us the desire to have our own children. We've experienced family and the love of family our entire lives and for this we are so grateful. Thank you to deMarco, my partner and my best friend. Thank you for being willing to join me on this journey and for being my balance. Thank you to Mary. Words will never be able to express my love and gratitude for you and the gift you have given. Thank you to Ben and Lexi and for the willingness to start this journey with us not knowing how it would unfold, but open to the possibilities. Thank you to the doctors, the nurses and all the staff who took these steps with us and affirmed us along the way. I particularly want to thank Dr. Pang from RSC and Dr. Robison, our OB-GYN. Thank you to Will Halm, Rich Vaughn and everyone at IFLC for handling and walking us through the legalities. Thank you to all of our friends and family, including our Unity family and other spiritual communities worldwide who have supported and encouraged us. You know who you are and we are so fortunate to have too many to mention personally. It truly takes a village. And, last but not least, thank you to Mr. Kurt Futrell who sponsored the publishing costs so this story can be told and shared with what I hope to be, MANY.

Some names have been changed throughout for confidentiality.

CONTENTS

FOREWORD

I was born into a Christian family. My father was a Seventh-day Adventist (SDA) minister. As a child growing up in the home of an SDA Church pastor, and attending an SDA school, I was indoctrinated with the fundamentals of SDA beliefs. So, how did I end up becoming a physician who is helping gay and lesbian couples build their families through Assisted Reproductive Technology (ART)?

As a young boy, I recognized that I was different from other boys: I had crushes on other boys. No amount of prayer, and not even my baptism at the age of ten years, took away those feelings. As a teenager, it dawned on me that these feelings were innate and were never going away. I realized that I needed to accept myself the way God created me. But why did God create me this way?

Putting my budding sexuality on the back burner, I focused my energies on my academic achievements. I graduated high school when I was sixteen years old and attended college in Vancouver, Canada. Three years later, I started medical school at the University of British Columbia when I was nineteen years old, graduating when I was twenty-three. After a one-year rotating internship in Toronto, Canada, I embarked on a residency in Obstetrics and Gynecology at the University of Toronto. It was during the third year of my residency that I discovered the subspecialty of reproductive endocrinology and infertility (REI). In vitro fertilization (IVF) was an emerging field at that time (the mid-1980s), and I decided that was what I wanted to do. I applied for a fellowship in REI at UCLA School of Medicine and was accepted, resulting in my move to Los Angeles, California. Following the completion of my two-year fellowship, I joined the faculty of the Loma Linda University School of Medicine, a Seventh-day Adventist institution, because I thought that I could serve the Lord there. But God had other plans for me...

Several years earlier, I had discovered SDA Kinship International, Inc., a peer support group for gay and lesbian Seventh-day Adventists. Kinship helped me to reconcile my sexuality with my spirituality. While living in Los Angeles, I discovered the Southern California Chapter of Physicians for Human Rights (SCPHR), which was later renamed the Gay and Lesbian Medical Association (GLMA). It was at a SCPHR meeting in the early 1990s that I met a cardiologist, Dr. Marcellin Simard, and his life partner, Will Halm, who was a lawyer. When they learned of my medical specialty, they invited me out to lunch one day to "pick my brain." They wanted to have children through surrogacy and had many questions for me. I explained to them how everything could be done, from the ART perspective, but I was unable to offer them my medical services because I was on the faculty at a Seventh-day Adventist medical school, which only allowed me to treat married heterosexual couples.

After three years at Loma Linda, God led me to Massachusetts, where I have lived since 1993. I joined the medical staff of an IVF program in the Boston area that would quickly become one of the largest and most successful IVF centers in the United States. Several years after I moved to Boston, I discovered that Marcellin and Will had gone on to have a child (and eventually three children) through egg donation and gestational surrogacy, and I was very pleased that they were able to find an IVF physician in the Los Angeles area who was able to provide them with ART services.

In 1997, I was appointed to be the medical director of the egg donation program at our IVF center. This meant that I managed all the IVF treatments that involved donor eggs and also those that involved gestational surrogates. The vast majority of our patients are heterosexual couples, but there are a few patients who are lesbian couples. I'll never forget the day my donor egg team coordinator came to me and said, "I just received a telephone call from this man…" She went on to describe a gay male couple who wanted to have a baby through egg donation and gestational surrogacy. She concluded by asking, "We don't do that here, do we?" And I replied, "We haven't done it before, but that doesn't mean that we don't or can't do it!" She breathed a sigh of relief and, with a smile, she said, "OK, I'll call him right back and schedule an appointment for them to meet with you."

Nicholas and Daniel (not their real names) were both thirty-one years old when they first approached me in June 1998. They had met in college and had been together as a couple for twelve years. They had always dreamed about having a family, and through their years together they had discussed and investigated various options. They ultimately decided that they wanted to have children through surrogacy. At that time, gay male couples who were having children through surrogacy were doing traditional surrogacy, which involved insemination of a surrogate who then conceived and, following the birth, she would give the baby to be adopted by the intended parents. Being an attorney, Nick was aware of the risks involved with doing traditional surrogacy. (At that time, there was a legal case involving surrogacy that was working its way up to the Massachusetts Supreme Judicial Court [SJC]. The Culliton case involved a married heterosexual couple who had used a gestational surrogate. In 1999, the MA SJC issued its decision on the Culliton case, and part of the ruling was that if a traditional surrogate changes her mind after the birth of the baby, she has the right to keep the baby as it is 50 percent her baby, having been conceived with her egg. However, if a gestational surrogate were to change her mind after the birth of the baby, she would have no legal right to keep the baby, as she did not provide the egg for conception of the baby.)

So, Nick and Dan decided to use donor eggs from an egg donor, combined with gestational surrogacy, instead of traditional surrogacy. At that time, even though gestational surrogacy was being done for many heterosexual couples (and most cases involved using eggs from the intended mother), this was a relatively novel concept for gay male couples. Egg donation combined with gestational surrogacy for male couples had only just begun in California, and very few cases had been done at the time.

Nick and Dan had called other IVF programs in the Boston area, none of which would consider treating them. They had also done a lot of groundwork before they met with me, having advertised and found, on their own, a woman who had agreed to be their gestational surrogate. They were truly pioneers, and I was thrilled to be in a position to help them build their family. Over the next six years, Nick and Dan went on to have three children through egg donation and gestational surrogacy—first a set of twins, one boy and one girl born in June 2000, followed later by another boy born in November 2004. During that period, I also helped another gay male couple have two children through egg donation and surrogacy, and they have a daughter who was born in April 2001 and a son who was born in September 2002.

In May 2004, Massachusetts became the first state in the United States to allow same-sex couples to marry, following the landmark MA SJC decision in November 2003. With the advent of marriage equality for same-sex couples, more and more gay male couples have decided to have children. While many choose adoption, those who desire genetic offspring have sought ART services to build their families. Since 2004, I have treated many gay male couples with egg donation and gestational surrogacy and, to date, 100 percent of them have been successful. Most of them live in Massachusetts, but there have also been couples from the neighboring New England states of New Hampshire and Connecticut, as well as from more distant states such as Maryland, Florida, and Texas. I have also treated gay male couples who have traveled to Boston from Europe and South America to have a baby through egg donation and gestational surrogacy.

Historically, lesbian couples have conceived easily with donor sperm, but within the past few years, several lesbian couples have approached me to do what I call "reciprocal IVF": one woman wants to provide her egg to create the embryo through IVF for her partner to carry the pregnancy, so that they can both participate biologically in the creation of their baby. What an incredible concept! As I look back, I can't help but wonder at all the above-described events that have led me to where I am now, to be able to help gay and lesbian couples build families with ART. I can't help but think of the story of Esther, and how God positioned her to be able to help her people in their time of need: "And who knows whether you have not come to the kingdom for such a time as this?" Esther 4:14 (RSV)

I met Jason and deMarco at the annual SDA Kinship Kampmeeting in California in July 2007. They had been invited to provide their music ministry, and I had been asked to provide a workshop in family-building options for gay and lesbian couples. They heard me describe how I have been helping many gay couples build families through ART, including my own family. (My husband

and I have two sons through egg donation and gestational surrogacy.) We live thousands of miles away from each other, but our paths crossed in California, eventually leading to the creation of their beautiful family. Coincidence? Or Providence?

This book describes Jason and deMarco's journey to parenthood. They share, with every other gay male couple that I've treated, their strong desire to become parents and their determination to persevere until they achieve their goal. From the technological perspective, their experience is unique among all the gay male couples that I've treated because they had to use the strategy of "embryo banking." This was necessary because they had an egg donor who had schedule restrictions—that is, she had a limited window of time to donate her eggs. Nor did they have a gestational surrogate available at the same time. Faced with this dilemma, I suggested that they proceed with the egg donation process, inseminate the eggs, and then freeze and "bank" the resulting embryos until they were able to identify a suitable gestational surrogate. No other gay male couple that I've treated has needed to use this strategy. But, as you will see, in spite of the numerous obstacles, their persistence paid off, and they have added two beautiful boys to their family.

My hope is that this book will inform gay and lesbian couples who would like to have children and inspire them to explore their options for having a family.

Samuel C. Pang, MD
Medical Director
Reproductive Science Center of New England
One Forbes Road
Lexington, MA 02421
www.GayIVF.com

PREFACE

As a little boy, I would daydream about being a dad. I loved children from the time I was a child. I loved watching newborn babies look around the room, wondering what was going through their mind. After all, what could they possibly be thinking? They have just come from the comfort of their warm, safe, and quiet environment and are suddenly introduced to the harsh, cold, and somewhat chaotic world in which they are about to live. Yet, somehow, they still smile with wonder and have an entire future of infinite possibility ahead of them.

There is nothing quite like the smell of a newborn baby. Unfortunately, I was too young to remember my two younger brothers, but I used to love holding my nieces and nephews while smelling the top of their head as they slept on my chest. To me, they represented the true innocence that we all had at one time.

When I was about seven years old, I decided that I wanted to be a pediatrician. I thought working with babies and children would be awesome! I remember thinking that I wanted to get married as soon as I graduated high school, and I wanted to have a baby soon after. I also knew I wanted A LOT of kids— probably six or more, although two girls and two boys seemed like the perfect scenario.

Although my parents were raised United Methodist, after moving to the Eastern Shore of Maryland when I was twelve years old, we began going to a Pentecostal Church of God. I'll never forget sitting in Sunday school when our teacher announced that our youth group had planned a group picnic at one of the congregant's ranch houses. The congregant had an in-the-ground pool. Our Sunday school teacher, Brother Lou, advised my class that according to the Church of God doctrine, there would be no mixed bathing. Being new to the Church of God, I raised my hand and asked, "What is mixed bathing?" Brother Lou went on to explain that our church did not allow boys and girls to swim together in any pool or at any beach. All of the boys would swim at one time, and the girls at another, "to avoid temptation."

When Brother Lou explained this, I suddenly felt a rush of excitement! I would get to be with all of the boys, together, in bathing suits, at one time! I had no idea why this excited me so, but I quickly figured it out.

I began realizing that I was not attracted to girls. I read a book that my mom gave me about teen adolescence, but I didn't feel like I related with anything the book said that I should be feeling, at least not with girls.

I didn't really understand what it all meant, but the older I got, the more I began realizing that I was gay. This marked a long journey of reconciliation that I won't go into a great deal in this book. Suddenly, though, I felt as if all of my dreams of one day having a family were gone.

I began my coming-out process at the age of twenty in college. It took at least four long years before I truly accepted myself. This was after reading as many books as I could get my hands on about the issue and being introduced to affirming churches. In 2001, at the age of twenty-six, I met my life partner. After being together for about five years and touring together as a duo in a band, we began to talk about starting a family and exploring our options. We knew fostering or adopting was an option, but when we discovered that we could, in fact, have children together who could be biological siblings, it felt as though my dream as a little boy was reborn in my soul. I'm thrilled to say that we have now been together for twelve years, and on May 23, 2011, we welcomed our beautiful twin sons, Mason and Noah.

When beginning our journey, I was amazed at how few resources there were regarding same-sex surrogacy. This field is new, and the research data available are sparse, so through the chapters of this book I hope to help intended parents walk through their journey—from the beginning of their process to the decisions that have to be made, from finding an egg donor and a surrogate to getting pregnant and finally bringing the baby or babies home for the first time. I bring to the forefront the many options, choices, and emotions that go along with this experience. I hope to offer insight to your experience while also sharing information with those couples or individuals who are considering surrogacy.

Although we still live in a society where many may disagree with same-sex marriage, same-sex adoption, and thus are almost sure to disagree with same-sex surrogacy, I believe the wisdom of scientists, medical doctors, and biologists is a gift from God. Just as chemotherapy gives someone the possibility of living his or her life to the fullest, I believe that IVF and surrogacy offer the possibility of having life's most precious gift: a child. This book is for anyone who has a dream of having a child and for whatever reason cannot do so traditionally. Gay or straight, single or partnered, this book is for you. For those who believe that their sexual orientation is that of homosexual, or for those who may not have the blessing of finding a life partner with whom to share their journey and choose to have a child through a surrogate as a single parent, this book is for you.

My goal is that this story will give hope to those young gay teens who may feel they have no chance for a family in their future. I believe it is important for everyone to know that they have the same opportunities as everyone else. Being different doesn't mean your life is over. It simply means that you may need to take another path to reach the ultimate destination—the ultimate joy.

PART I

OUR STORY

ABOUT US

It was right around our five-year anniversary that the conversation began about whether or not deMarco and I wanted kids. I had always loved kids, but I didn't really know how deMarco felt. When meeting someone, I always hoped that having a family would be a priority, but I wasn't really sure what that would look like considering our "situation." We had been touring four of those five years in a band together. We sang in many different venues, but our ultimate dream was to be an out pop duo, touring with a live band, performing as a double act with a well-known artist. We didn't necessarily need to be performing in stadiums, but we wanted to be performing in professional venues where we didn't have to produce our own shows.

Many of our venues were churches. The churches would offer their space to us to hold our shows, but we'd open the concerts to the entire community. Our message, although often considered inspirational, was very plain and simple: "The greatest thing you'll ever learn is just to love and be loved in return." We believe all any of us in this human family desire is to love and to be loved.

I've always loved singing, and I've known very little other than singing. I sang as a child with my mom. I sang in college and was on scholarship traveling to youth camps, performing with a band, and recruiting for the college. I graduated college and toured with a Christian band, and when I left the Christian band because of "coming out," I began touring as a solo artist sharing my story of reconciling with being a gay man and believing this was exactly who I was created to be.

When I met deMarco, he was pursuing his own music career, and we decided that if we were going to be together, we might as well tour together, so we formed a duo, and I went by my middle name, Jason, meaning "Healer," and we became known as "Jason & deMarco."

As much as I love singing, I have always had tons of other interests. I like so many things that it's sometimes hard to decide what I like most. I've always thought once the touring was done, I'd work at a university, run my own nonprofit, go into real estate, become a minister, and the list goes on and on. However, I never heard deMarco talk about doing anything other than singing. His career was his main focus. He had moved from Toronto, Canada, to Los Angeles—knowing no one—to pursue his dream. After finding an agent, being cast in a few national commercials, booking a touring theatrical show in Italy, and finally feeling like things were taking off, his commitment and devotion to his career were stronger than ever.

Through our touring, many people often asked, "So, when are you guys going to have kids?" And, of course, we'd reply with the typical response: "Well, we keep trying but nothing happens!" It always got a laugh, but somehow it didn't feel funny to me anymore. It left me feeling sad and, at times, even angry. It didn't seem fair that I couldn't have a biological child with this man whom I adored and with whom I wanted to spend the rest of my life. I had constantly heard about teenage pregnancy, abortion, and the number of children needing homes. How could someone ever give up or abandon his or her child? Why are there so many people desperate to have children, while others want to get rid of them? It seemed implausible to me and, quite honestly, unfair.

And in my private moments with God, I'd think, *Why?*

I had heard about surrogacy—and the horror stories that went along with it. I remembered hearing how a woman in New York had gotten pregnant as a surrogate but when the baby was born decided she didn't want to give it up. To my understanding, it's for this reason surrogacy is illegal in the state of New York, even to this day. Other than these few negative stories, I really wasn't educated on the process of surrogacy. I couldn't imagine a woman going through something so traumatic for someone else.

Then, everything seemed to change and fall into place. I went to a friend's picnic and sat next to a gay man who had a son. We talked about his experience, and I was in awe. He was in his early forties and had always dreamed of having kids. He kept waiting to find a life partner and finally decided to begin his family as a single dad. His friend had offered to be a gestational surrogate for him.

I wasn't aware that there were two types of surrogates: a traditional and a gestational carrier. A traditional surrogate is willing to also be the biological mother of the child she will carry. Gestational surrogates get pregnant through IVF only and have no biological connection to the baby, meaning a separate egg donor is required, and the fertilization process is done in a clinic. Most agencies recommend a gestational carrier simply because there seems to be less emotional concern for the surrogate if she has no biological connection to the child she has carried and ultimately gives away after birth.

This man I was speaking with had worked with an egg donor agency and chose eggs from hundreds of women's profiles. He could narrow it down by hair color, eye color, ethnicity, education, career, talents, and the list goes on and on. After choosing the eggs from the egg donor agency, he went to a fertility doctor who took the eggs and fertilized them with this man's sperm. At that time, any eggs that fertilized were considered zygotes or blastocysts, which ultimately become embryos. The doctor took the most viable blastocysts and implanted it (or them) into the surrogate. Within ten days, he found out he was pregnant! The procedure is obviously much more detailed, but sitting there at the picnic table with him, I suddenly felt a rush of excitement and joy!

I looked at his little boy playing in the pool, and I watched the two of them interacting with one another, and it was truly beautiful. This man didn't let anyone dictate whether or not he could have a child. He had a dream of being a dad, and he made it happen.

Soon after, deMarco and I performed at an affirming Seventh-day Adventist conference (neither myself nor deMarco are Adventists, but we take our music and message anywhere the door opens) where later we were seated at a dinner table. On my left was a fertility lawyer, and on my right was a fertility doctor. Let's just say that by the end of the evening, I had asked every question that could be asked, and my neck was sore from twisting, going back and forth between the lawyer and the doctor.

When we left the event, I looked at deMarco and said, "I think we're getting the neon signs." He smiled and agreed. It became obvious that this was our calling. We both agreed that if it were truly meant to happen, an egg donor and a surrogate would come into our lives. We had just discovered, after speaking with the doctor and lawyer at dinner, the average costs involved with going through an agency to find an egg donor and a surrogate, and we realized we weren't in any position to afford that; after all, we lived primarily on love offerings and CD sales. We also agreed that perhaps in the future we'd be in a place where we could afford it, and so we would wait for that time.

2

Choosing Our Egg Donor

Not long after our experience at the dinner table with the fertility doctor and lawyer, we were in New Jersey visiting our good friends Ben and Lexi, a straight couple with two children at the time, pregnant with their third. We typically visited each other once or twice a year, and on this visit we began talking about our own possibility of having a child. They immediately lit up when we told them; they thought we would make incredible parents.

In the midst of our joking around about how we were going to get pregnant, the conversation turned more serious, and they agreed that they were open to helping us make this happen. Although we weren't ready to talk details yet, we felt like this was a strong possibility and continued the conversation over the next two years until deMarco and I were certain we were ready to move forward. Both Ben and Lexi decided they didn't want more children after their third and, to our amazement, Ben chose to get a vasectomy rather than Lexi's getting her tubes tied so that she would be able to do this for us. We were blown away by their love and generosity, and still are to this day.

Unfortunately, after Lexi's third pregnancy, there were some complications, and she was told she could no longer carry a child. I remember getting the phone call; she was devastated. We assured her that it was OK and that she needed to take care of herself and do what needed to be done. They needed to cauterize her uterus—that is, burn the inside of her uterine wall—which would, of course, ruin any chance of an embryo ever being able to attach.

Lexi told us she could still donate her eggs, but we would need to find another person to carry for us—a surrogate. We weren't completely sure how possible this was, so I called the doctor whom I had met at the event. Not only was this possible, he'd said, but this was preferred. They preferred the surrogate, or gestational carrier, to not be the biological egg donor. He explained that when a surrogate doesn't have a biological connection to the baby she is carrying, it is believed to be a smoother transition, particularly emotionally, to give the baby to the intended parents after birth. This made total sense, and we were relieved! However, we still couldn't afford to go through an agency to find a surrogate. This alone could cost anywhere between $30,000 and $100,000, depending on the agency. Again, we felt that we would take it one step at a time and trust that if this were supposed to happen, it would.

We wanted the egg donor to be someone we knew. We liked that we already knew everything about Lexi. Plus, Lexi and Ben were both clear that they would desire no parental role in the child's life.

Some people find this extremely difficult to understand—that Lexi could have a child "out there" in the world and be OK with it. Some are even more amazed that a woman's husband would be OK with knowing there is a child in the world that his wife had with someone else.

Fortunately, Lexi and Ben were both extremely open-minded people. All they knew is that deMarco and I would make incredible parents, and they felt no biological responsibility to these children. They saw this as a precious gift they could offer us and, being parents themselves, they understood just how precious this gift was.

Some people may prefer an egg donor who is anonymous, and this is understandable. It really is completely up to the individual, or couple. I felt extremely blessed that Lexi and Ben would be in our lives, even if we saw them only occasionally, and they would get to see our children grow up. In addition, our children would have two half brothers and a half sister whom we know and have watched grow up!

3

Choosing Our Clinic

A nother year passed. We were touring extensively and knew that if we wanted to begin a family, our lives would have to change drastically; yet, we felt as if we were getting close to being ready. Being in a band and traveling the world was a wonderful thing, but it didn't lend itself to having a child.

We decided to call the doctor we had met at the event, Dr. Pang, and begin the conversation. We wanted someone we trusted and someone we knew would be extremely gay friendly throughout this process. Although Dr. Pang and the clinic were in Boston, it was important to us that we work with a clinic that was completely supportive in our decisions. We also felt that it was no mistake that we met him at the event where we performed and made the connection.

At this time, I was thirty-two, deMarco was thirty-one, and Lexi was thirty-one. Dr. Pang recommended that we not wait much longer as it is not recommended that you use eggs, or harvest eggs, from a woman who is over the age of thirty-two. This doesn't mean that you can't; it simply means that once a woman reaches thirty-two, her eggs may become less viable when fertilizing. This was shocking news for us since we weren't ready to get pregnant yet; however, Dr. Pang also shared that even though this procedure is fairly new, studies show that the fertilized eggs, or embryos, have been successfully frozen up to ten years and still were viable when transferring to the surrogate, achieving pregnancy.

In other words, we could move forward with the harvesting of the eggs and fertilizing and then freeze the fertilized eggs, or embryos, until we were ready to transfer after finding a surrogate. We would have up to ten years to do this. This seemed the most logical thing to do, and although we didn't have the money even for the harvesting and fertilizing, we decided to move forward. Thank God for credit cards! Looking over the numbers, we knew the average for this procedure would probably run $15,000–$20,000, and we were fortunate enough to have a credit limit between us to cover this amount.

We talked with Lexi and Ben, and we all agreed to move forward. Boston was in driving distance from Lexi in New Jersey, so we scheduled the consult with the clinic. Lexi and Ben met with the psychologist separately, and then deMarco and I met with the same psychologist. Then, we all met together. Lexi had to take an array of tests, including blood tests and personality tests. We were pretty amazed at the detail involved in "approving" someone to be our egg donor. Ultimately, I believe it would have been our choice regardless, but they strongly advise, and I do believe they have the right to refuse if they do not feel the situation is healthy for all involved. Fortunately, we didn't have any problems, and they gave us the green light.

4

SCRAMBLED EGGS

On April 1, 2007, we arrived at the clinic. Lexi was by herself because Ben was working out of state. She looked great, and although she said she felt like she was three months' pregnant, she was in good spirits. She had been taking her hormone shots for approximately thirty days, which enabled her to release many eggs at once. Another hormone prevented her from getting her period where they would release, thus the reason she was bloated and felt pregnant. The more eggs, the merrier, as we'd have more to harvest and, hopefully, fertilize. We were told that the average number of mature eggs retrieved is usually six to eight.

While Lexi was being prepped to be mildly sedated, deMarco and I went to the waiting room. About thirty minutes later, they came and got us. We went in and saw Lexi, who was still pretty out of it. The doctor immediately told us that he was able to retrieve thirteen mature eggs! We were ecstatic. This meant that all thirteen eggs could be used to attempt fertilization.

deMarco and I had agreed to split the eggs evenly, so with thirteen there was an extra. My birthday is April 5th, and deMarco told me that I could have the extra. So, they would attempt fertilizing seven of the eggs with my sperm and six of the eggs with deMarco's sperm.

Next, we had to decide whether we wanted to use intracytoplasmic sperm injection (ICSI), which is a fancy way of saying "inject the sperm directly into the egg." ICSI is an effective method to fertilize eggs in the IVF lab after they have been retrieved from the female. The other option was to simply put the eggs and our sperm into a dish and let them do their thing. However, with ICSI, they choose the strongest sperm—that is, the best shape, the fastest swimmers, and the overall healthiest in appearance—and manually insert them into the eggs. This procedure would cost us at least a couple extra thousand dollars, but after spending the amount of money and coming this far, we felt it was the best option.

At this point, we were sent back to the hotel and told to wait. We would receive a call the next morning and be told the results of how many eggs fertilized overnight after being injected with our sperm. But injecting the sperm didn't necessarily mean fertilizing the egg.

As you can imagine, it was not easy waiting. Lexi felt wonderful and was relieved that her part was complete! So, we celebrated. We probably drank four bottles of wine, had a beautiful dinner, and went back to our rooms ready to sleep the night away. That evening is a memory I will always hold very special.

The next morning, feeling a bit hung over, we had breakfast. That's when we received a personal phone call from the doctor. Usually the nurse calls, but Dr. Pang was an angel and called us personally. He explained that six of the eggs took with my sperm, and six of the eggs took with deMarco's. It was a tie. We all laughed and were quite overwhelmed. We had succeeded!

They would freeze all of the embryos. There would be a banking fee of $85 per month to store the eggs. Since it would be at least three years before we would try to get pregnant, this was obviously an investment. In that moment, finding out we had embryos, it was tempting to move forward right away and get pregnant. But we knew we weren't ready. Plus, we hadn't found our baby mama! This was going to be the next big step, and perhaps the most challenging. However, we had faith and reminded ourselves how everything had fallen into place thus far. So, we trusted the rest would as well.

5

Finding Our Baby Mama

Over the following year after harvesting, our life began to take some interesting turns. I'd always believed that once you set something in motion, the Universe aligns and completely supports it.

Although we had achieved success in the secular pop music world, we were still performing a lot in churches on Sundays. At that time, we were heading to Houston to record with our producer, and our booking assistant contacted the Unity church in Houston to ask if they would be interested in having us come sing. We often found Unity churches to be much more hesitant to meet our financial requests, but this Unity pretty much said yes to all of our standard requests, and before we knew it we were booked.

We had also begun working with Atlantis Cruises. This company charted full ships, and there were anywhere from two to four thousand gay boys, with a few lesbians here and there, floating on the open seas for seven or more days. Atlantis hired us to come on board and do two shows. It was a really fun time and much needed after touring in churches for over six years. (Don't get me wrong; we loved what we were doing, and the churches had been so supportive, but we felt as if we were losing our youth.) We hardly had any time to just hang out with friends our age because we were always touring. Getting on the cruise ship was downtime for us; it allowed us to meet some really fun people. We were able to be young and have fun while getting paid for it! And we had the opportunity to travel to some places we probably wouldn't have seen otherwise, so it was a great experience.

We were supposed to sing at Unity in Houston on Sunday morning to help promote the concert we'd be holding the following Friday night. This was a little unusual for us because we normally sang in a Sunday morning service to help promote a Sunday evening concert. But this was how this church operated, and we figured they knew best. Unfortunately, our cruise ported in San Juan and, due to weather in the Northeast, all flights had been canceled. Basically, the planes couldn't get out of the Northeast to get to us. We were able to get a flight to Miami, but that would be the farthest we could get, and they didn't have any flights out of Miami until Monday morning due to the hundreds of passengers and flights that had been canceled. We tried everything, but there was simply no way we could get to Houston in time for our Sunday morning appearance.

We called the music director at Unity to tell him about our situation. It was obviously unfortunate, but they agreed to keep the Friday night concert, and we would hope for the best. It's sometimes hard to get people to come out to hear someone they've never heard, so our singing in the Sunday morning services was pretty important to introduce us to the congregation and entice them to come back Friday night.

We showed up and performed Friday night. We had a great turnout, and we really connected with the community. Afterward, two staff members approached me and said they could really envision me working at the church with their youth and young adults. When they said this, I felt a huge *pop*. What no one had known was that several months prior, I had begun envisioning that we would find a church that was willing to hire us two weekends per month and allow us to travel two weekends per month. I wasn't specific in "where." I just felt this would bring more balance to our lives. It would prepare us to take some time off from touring to begin our family.

When we left Unity that night, I asked deMarco if he had felt "anything" special with this community; he said he had. For me, this was a huge confirmation. However, we were living in Los Angeles, and deMarco made it very clear that he had no desire to move to Texas, so I put the idea on the backburner and sat with it for a few months.

During this time, when we were traveling to Houston to record with our producer, I began realizing that we were spending so much on hotels that it would perhaps be a good investment to purchase something and rent a room out to our producer and his partner. We would have a place to stay, and it would practically pay for itself. So, we did! We purchased a cute little townhouse near our studio.

Following our visit to Unity, I kept feeling a pull toward the ladies' telling me what they envisioned. My degree is in sociology with an emphasis in student counseling, and since coming out I had not worked much with youths or young adults. Most of the Metropolitan Community Churches we traveled to had a congregation with a median age of fifty. Although we received a lot of e-mails from young people, and talked about teenage suicide and teenage homelessness within the GLBT community, we didn't have the opportunity to work with them very often. This has always been a strong passion of mine, so the thought of doing this at Unity excited me.

During one of our trips to Houston, when I was vacuuming the townhouse, I remember thinking, *Why aren't we living here?* Although our apartment in Los Angeles was beautiful, we were so cramped there. Our closets were overflowing with CDs, T-shirts, and other merchandise. We traveled almost every weekend, and many flights were to the East Coast. We spent hours on planes and were getting tired. We had toured for six years and averaged five days in Los Angeles per month, while being on the road the other days. I had been doing this for three years before deMarco joined me and, quite honestly, I was exhausted. In that moment, I said to deMarco, "I think we should move to Houston." Again, he was not favorable, but this time I didn't just say I *thought* we should. I said I felt we were meant to move to Houston. I also intuitively felt that we were going to meet some key people living in Houston, and I was confident one of them would be our surrogate.

It wasn't a quick decision, but eventually deMarco agreed to consider the possibility. I put together a proposal to send to the minister at Unity and shared our interest in joining their staff, while also continuing our touring. I'm not sure why, but I was quite shocked when he e-mailed back saying he was very interested and that he would like to meet with us to discuss this in greater depth. This was a two-thousand member church, primarily straight. That they would be open to hiring two openly gay men was a big deal.

It just so happened that we were heading to a Unity conference in Kansas City, and the minister of the Unity in Houston was also going to be there with his wife and executive director. We planned a lunch meeting, and so it was. This would be a huge shift for us, traveling only two weekends per month, and although we'd be taking a financial cut, we felt it would be worth having more stability.

We had our lunch meeting, and within days the church had agreed to our terms. It was pretty much a done deal. The specifics would be dealt with on another visit to Houston, but we were moving forward.

Within a few weeks, another visit to Houston had been planned. We walked into the minister's office where we met several other staff members. One of those staff members was the youth and family director, Mary. I remember meeting Mary because she reminded me of my cousin, Eileen. She had a strange familiarity. She had red hair, and I could tell she had a fun personality, although it took a little time to help her feel comfortable enough to share it. She got flustered easily. While I felt she was excited about my coming on board, I also felt she was a bit dissatisfied. Later I learned that Mary was raised in Unity, and when she found out that I had come from the Pentecostal background, she thought I wasn't going to be "new thought" enough.

As woo-woo as I can get, and as open as I am to all spiritual paths, I've never hidden the fact that i love jesus! However, what Mary didn't realize was that although I consider myself a very spiritual person, I am probably one of the least religious people you'll ever meet. My spirituality has expanded radically over the past ten years, and in time I knew I would appease Mary's concerns.

As I shared my vision for the church and for the youth ministry and talked about some of the programming I envisioned, I could tell Mary was excited and got me. She was totally cool with the gay issue, which was another huge relief. Here we were at a large mainstream church with over two thousand congregants, and they were hiring an openly gay man, and his partner, to work with their youth program. I admired the minister for this. He told me from the beginning, "If anyone has an issue with it, they can come see me." I thought that was awesome.

In the meeting it was decided our joining the staff would be announced on a Sunday the church has in November called "Celebration Sunday." Our start date, however, would not be until the first of the year, January of 2008.

Over the last few months of the year, we continued our traveling and prepared for our move to Houston. Fortunately, the house was already furnished, and our producer and his partner had decided to move out. We all felt it would be best, and deMarco and I wanted to have our own space to really begin creating a "home."

This was the first huge step for us in preparing for our family. In having children we would not be able to tour the way we had our entire career, at least for the first six months or first year, if not more. Of course, having a nanny travel with us was an option, but we felt we wouldn't want to be on the road being dads, at least for a few years. So, moving to Houston, taking the job at the church, and touring less all seemed to be moving us in the right direction.

Our early transition at the church went fairly smoothly. There were some ideas that didn't work, but more that did. We worked at the church for five years and will always treasure our time there.

After living in Houston for about a year and a half, we met a girl at a conference where we were performing in San Antonio. She was also from Houston. Within the first five minutes of our conversation, surrogacy came up. This was a little strange, but we both laughed it off. I said, "Well, it's funny you mention surrogacy because we are looking for a surrogate!" This began a conversation that lasted several months. We had just begun the process, and Kelly had filled out the paperwork and sent it to the Reproductive Science Center. But when she came back from one of her extended trips, she announced that she had met someone, that she thought it might be a serious relationship, and that he was not comfortable with her being a surrogate. In addition, she had entered into a custody situation with her ex and her six-year-old son, and she felt the stress would not be good for a surrogacy. We agreed and, although we were disappointed, we trusted the right person would come along at the right time.

During this time our relationship with Mary, the youth director at Unity, continued growing stronger. Mary was becoming the sister I never had. She began helping us with our music business, handling our online websites, and dealing with our VIP and Street Team members. She also began helping me with my young adult programming. We both shared a passion for Unity and what we could do to grow the movement. We loved creating together!

At a restaurant one evening, after Mary and I had finished eating, she said, "I have something I want to tell you, but I don't know if I should." Of course, this only made me want her to tell me. She said she had had a dream, and she felt like she might be the one who was supposed to have our children. My first reaction was, "What?" Mary didn't enjoy being pregnant and had told me about her experience. Mary was also a redhead, and I didn't know how temperamental she might be during pregnancy (no offense to redheads). I also wondered how it would affect our friendship, how the church would feel, and so on. All of these thoughts quickly raced through my mind, and I basically laughed and said, "I love you for being willing, but I don't think so."

As deMarco and I continued our conversation about having the baby or babies, Mary often heard our desire to begin a family. Being a children's and youth director, she obviously had a love for children and understood how precious a gift they are. Sure, they can sometimes drive you crazy, but they are such a gift. I'm not sure what it was exactly, but our having a family resonated with Mary. We all felt it. We all knew it.

I was hosting a young adult conference, and a young lady at the conference named Katie from Dallas attended. She was my team leader at the Unity in Dallas, and I had exchanged e-mails with her and met her at a few other retreats. She was rooming with Mary, and one morning during the conference she came up and said, "I had the weirdest dream last night. I dreamed I was having yours and deMarco's baby!" Of course, I laughed and said, "Well, we're looking for a surrogate." This began a few long, difficult months.

We agreed to move forward with Katie, who was only twenty-two. The clinic advised us against it, but we felt Katie was mature for her age, and after flying to Boston with Katie and undergoing the same psychological evaluation that we'd had with Lexi, the clinic agreed to move forward.

There were so many issues with this situation that I don't even know where to begin. At first everything seemed great, and we were all excited. I could tell Katie really wanted to help make this a reality for us, and we were happy to be able to help her through a tough time. She was a single mother of a seven-year-old son, had gotten pregnant at fifteen, was in college, and could really use some extra money. We didn't have a lot to budget, but we offered her $10,000 to be our surrogate. In addition, we were purchasing her health insurance through her school for a year, and we were going to cover all of her medical expenses surrounding the pregnancy. We had also agreed to pay her childcare if she needed to hire someone to help with her son.

A few red flags appeared early on. After our meeting with the clinic and into the process, Katie told me that she was legally married. Typically, a husband has to consent to his wife's being a surrogate. She explained that the marriage was for immigration purposes only and that she and her friend had never even lived together. I didn't see this as a problem, but legally her "husband" would have to sign the surrogacy contract relinquishing all rights to the baby or babies when born. She said this wasn't a problem. We hired a fertility law firm out of Los Angeles—National Fertility Law—and they began all of the paperwork.

Prior to filling out the paperwork and hiring the attorney, I had a heart to heart with Katie and gave her a way out. I told her that perhaps this involved more than she had expected (which I know it did) and that we would understand if she needed to reconsider. She asked for a few days, and when we talked she said that she wanted to move forward. So, we did. I really think Katie wanted to help us become dads. Every time we'd talk, she'd say, "You're going to be daddies!" But I just don't think she understood what would actually be involved in making this a reality.

The main issues had to do with her school schedule. Katie hadn't realized how many appointments were necessary during the surrogacy process. She had to go for a sonohystogram, missing a Monday of class. The professor allowed students to miss only two classes during a semester, and then their letter grade would be decreased per absence. It just so happened that Katie's doctor scheduled appointments on Mondays. So, we had to find another doctor's office who would offer appointments other days of the week. Regardless, Katie was missing class, and she was concerned about her schooling.

Katie also wanted to give birth in a birthing center rather than a hospital. She had found a birthing center very close to her university and talked with them about our arrangement. We wanted to make sure they were supportive. We also wanted to make sure they would accept her insurance and treat her no differently than if she were a woman walking in who just found out she was pregnant, rather than filing any paperwork showing that she was a surrogate. This was mainly for insurance purposes. We figured the less the insurance company knew, the better. We wanted to avoid any chance that they would try to deny coverage. The birthing center was very supportive. I spoke with the director who said they would file the insurance, and even if the insurance for some reason declined coverage, the total costs for birthing in their facility would be no greater than $5000, assuming there were no complications. Although $5000 is a lot of money, it was manageable.

Going into this with Katie, we were very clear that our ultimate desire was to end up with one embryo each that could be transferred, giving us both a chance to have a biological child and having fraternal twins. It would be one of each! And even more amazing, they would be biological siblings through Lexi, the egg donor. However, the birth center informed us that they only delivered single births. If a woman was pregnant with twins, they would refer her to the hospital. We asked if they made exceptions, and they said it was rare. Katie really had her heart set on this center, but we really had our heart set on transferring one embryo each, giving us a chance for twins. This began another long process of my feeling like I was trying to convince Katie to be open to having twins and following our desires rather than her own.

Because we had no idea how many embryos would even survive when we thawed to transfer, all of this was so hypothetical. Our conversations went in circles, it seemed. I could feel Katie's fears arise. I'd talk her through it, remind her of the costs of what we had done thus far, and tell her we didn't want to miss an opportunity to transfer one of each if we had it; and I ultimately suggested we leave it up to the Universe. I remember saying, "Look, if we're only supposed to transfer one, then only one will be viable. If we're supposed to transfer two, then we'll each have one." Finally, that's exactly what we decided. But what if there were two viable embryos of only one of us? Would we still only transfer one knowing that even though we could refreeze the second viable embryo, it would become less viable with each thaw and we'd have to pay for an entire new cycle? Yet, we also knew if we transferred two of the same person, we could end up with two babies—both biologically either my or deMarco's. But what if we only transferred one, refroze the second, and the one didn't take? We would always wonder, *What if?* No matter what we decided, there would be a lot of what-ifs in this process. We ultimately decided the only way we would transfer two embryos is if it were one of each; otherwise, only one would be transferred. Katie agreed.

After going over these decisions with the clinic and putting together our contract with the attorney, several other issues arose. First, Reproductive Science Center required birth records from a surrogate for any prior children. Katie couldn't find her birth records for her son. The doctor she had delivered with was no longer in practice. Fortunately, the Reproductive Science Center waived this request. Second, we weren't aware that a sonohystogram was required. They weren't willing to waive this. When Katie went for her sonohystogram, first they had to do a consult, which was $100. The sonohystogram was going to be $400. The doctor's office did sonohystograms only two days per week; on both days Katie had a heavy class load. I received a call from Katie saying that the doctor's office had called to remind her of her appointment, but she wouldn't be able to do it because of a test. She said she had called the doctor's office but had to leave a message. Apparently, the doctor's office didn't get the message. When rescheduled, Katie missed the second appointment, and the doctor's office said that they would not reschedule with her and that she would need to go to another doctor. They would refund the $400, but they would not refund the $100 consultation fee. Katie was very upset about this and called me crying. I calmed her down and explained that it would all be OK. We could have fought it, but at this point we felt it would be better for her to go to another doctor. This wasn't the attitude we wanted during this process. So, I called around and found a doctor's office that would take Katie on a Friday; on that day she had only two classes in the afternoon. I explained the situation to the office. They advised that she would need to come in for a consult, and I explained that she had just done a consult at the other doctor's office and questioned whether they could simply transfer the consult. They said they couldn't, so we had to start from scratch. Some of these issues may seem small, but when you are stretched to the limit financially and emotionally, they add up quickly.

Katie was fearful of the exam, and it took another two weeks before she finally did it. We had only a few days left until the Reproductive Science Center's deadline for the results or they would not move forward. The good news was, after all was said and done, Katie's uterus looked in perfect shape, and we were good to go.

Katie also had a huge fear of needles. When she saw the shots she would need to give herself, she freaked out. Fortunately, she had a friend who lived a few doors down, and her friend offered to give her the shots. These were Lupron shots; the needle is the same needle people use for insulin. When she saw the progesterone shots she would have to take for eight to ten weeks, every day, the Lupron shots looked like nothing! We were told the progesterone could be taken in other forms, but the most organic way was through the shots. It was an oil-based liquid, and this was also the preferred method, giving the best chance for absorption. Many miscarriages are the result of low levels of progesterone, so it's extremely important that the carrier take these shots seriously. Katie agreed to the shots and would begin taking the Lupron about thirty days prior to transfer. She would then take the progesterone three days prior to transfer and continue through the confirmation of pregnancy. If pregnant, she would continue for another eight to ten weeks.

A few days into beginning her shots, Katie found out her son had been sexually assaulted by her best friend's older son, who had some mental challenges. Katie reported it to the police, and this impacted their friendship. Her friend ended up trying to get Katie kicked out of the college. Because of this situation, Katie missed more class and considered taking incompletes during the semester. However, doing so would cancel her insurance that we had purchased for her, and she would lose her scholarship and housing on campus. We couldn't afford a delivery in a hospital with no insurance, and we had already spent almost $2000 on her insurance that would be canceled if she withdrew from school. We were obviously concerned about her, but we were also concerned with all of this stress and how it could affect the surrogacy, or the success of the transfer. We had heard that stress is not good for implantation. We had limited attempts and had spent tens of thousands of dollars already and couldn't afford to take any chances. Yet, we had come so far and been through so much. How could we stop now? We were less than a month away from transferring, something we had been dreaming about for almost three years.

I reached out to the one person I truly felt understood how important this was to me, the one who knew all involved and had been so supportive, the one who was holding the vision for us, with us, and the one who, I felt, had been with us through the entire journey—Mary. When we had decided to work with Katie, Mary was happy for us, but there was also a huge sadness. The day Katie came up and told me about her dream, Mary had gone over to the steps and began to cry. When I walked over and asked, "What's wrong?" she said "I don't understand why I feel so strongly that I'm supposed to do this for you." Her life at the time wasn't in a place to offer this. Her husband was not supportive. They were coparenting their two children but hadn't been living as husband and wife for quite some time. They were good friends, and they both loved their children and wanted their kids to have a home with a family, something both of them did not have. Even though Mary felt her husband didn't need to be involved in her decision in the beginning, she quickly realized that without his support, this would not be possible. Legally, the husband of a carrier is required to sign the contract to relinquish any rights. In addition, if she were to get pregnant, especially with twins, there is a chance of bed rest, and she would need her husband's support with the kids. When she mentioned it to him, he basically said, "Hell no!" So, even though she felt she was supposed to do this, she could not commit. What she could commit to was supporting us, being a friend to Katie, and loving us all through the process.

After Katie informed me of her son's being molested, things continued to spiral downhill. The shots were affecting Katie in a very negative way. She became depressed. She wasn't doing well in school. She was tired. She was crying at the drop of a hat. She couldn't sleep. Everything was falling apart, and we had only a few weeks left to transfer. I tried to remind her that this would pass and that we'd have a beautiful baby! She would always say, "Aw, you're going to be daddies," which would reassure me, but deep down I had a knot in my stomach. deMarco knew very little about any of this. He was keeping busy with business as usual. I felt like a life coach talking Katie through every negative situation, a researcher trying to understand side effects and what hormones actually do, a lawyer having to read over these contracts and agreements, a doctor having to learn about the processes, and a spiritual man standing on my faith and principles. It wasn't easy.

Two weeks prior to transferring, Katie called. Her father had committed suicide. He lived in the Pacific Northwest, and although he had left her and her mother when she was little, she had reconnected with him just a few years prior and was trying to establish a relationship. She had a lot of resentment toward him and didn't consider herself close to him by any means, but this was obviously a shock, and she was going to be flying out for the funeral. Obviously this meant missing more school, and she had already asked for grace from her professors for her missed days of classes due to doctor appointments.

I didn't know what to say. Did this mean it was over? We were two weeks away from transferring. I asked her how she felt, and she said she had no plans of not moving forward, but she did agree that she was an emotional mess. We offered to fly her to her dad's funeral because she didn't have the funds to do so. I told her to take some time and really think things through and let us know how she felt when she returned. She also agreed to continue her shots.

Within the week we got the call from Katie. Again, we were less than two weeks out from transferring, and I'll never forget her words. She said, "Guys, I still want to do this for you, but I really feel like I need a few months to process everything. I don't think I am in any position to get pregnant, or healthy enough right now to carry a child." My heart sank. I was devastated. We were so close, and now she was asking us to wait a few months. My first reaction was, "Katie, no!" But after hearing her reasoning, I couldn't help but agree to everything she said. It was April, and we agreed that we would wait until June or July.

Somewhere deep down I knew this was the end of this journey with Katie; however, she was our only hope, so we agreed. It was all of the little things that had taken such an emotional toll on me. I can't even remember how many times I had to change flight reservations to the clinic in Boston for all of us, trying to coordinate our schedule with her schedule, arriving at the same time, departing at the same time, renting a car, rebooking a car, renting a hotel, canceling a hotel, rebooking a hotel. Thank God for Southwest Airlines who didn't charge any change fees. Plus, I could easily rebook a reservation online with credit from a canceled reservation. Again, things that may seem simple or small, but took a great amount of time and energy.

I had to e-mail the Reproductive Science Center to schedule a new date and make sure Dr. Pang was available. We had to figure out a new schedule and start Katie on the hormones from scratch, which meant more money. It was exhausting. Those were the moments when I thought, *Why aren't we adopting?*

I had always wanted to adopt. (Ironically, deMarco and I **ARE** now adoptive parents as well as biological parents due to Texas not allowing two males to be listed as parents on a birth certificate. We had to go through second-parent adoption with Mason and Noah, each adopting the others biological child.) I had always been very open to fostering and adopting. However, when the connections happened to make the surrogacy option a reality so quickly, I had to believe it was because it was what we were supposed to be doing. Maybe you don't believe in "supposed to." Perhaps everything is simply what it is. Perhaps it is completely meaningless. But in my life, everyone knows my favorite phrase is "It's a sign!" To this day, I am always looking for clues, for neon signs. We had been given so many that there was no possibility this wasn't what we were meant to be doing. Everything up to this point had gone so smoothly, so perfect! Why was this happening now?

Meanwhile, deMarco and I were planning our wedding. When we decided to move forward with the surrogacy, we had already decided to have our wedding ceremony on May 15, 2010. We had legally married in Los Angeles on August 22, 2008, prior to Prop 8, and we are one of the legally married couples who remain legal in the state of California. However, after our legal marriage at the courthouse and a small reception with our Los Angeles friends at the restaurant where we met, we decided we'd have an actual ceremony after we had time to plan and do things the way we had always dreamed. It took almost two years, but we had finally picked the date, picked the place, and the plans were in motion.

I remember sitting in our hot tub and saying to deMarco, "Honey, are we sure we want to do all of this in the same year? We are getting married, trying to get pregnant, and shooting a new music video, all of which costs a lot of money and takes a lot of time and energy." I had even suggested that we foster first. "What if we foster kids short term? This way, we'll have some experience in parenting and be better prepared for having babies of our own." This did not resonate with deMarco at all. Clearly, he wanted to move forward with surrogacy first. He had always said that he wanted to have our biological children first and then foster or adopt. I'm not sure why he felt so strongly about this, but I respected his decision and trusted it. When deMarco felt something strongly, I usually took notice because he's one of the most laid back, non-opinionated people I've ever met.

So, we were originally going to transfer with Katie April 26. We planned the shooting of our music video the first week of May, and our wedding would be May 15. Yes, not only did we do all of this in the same year, but we did it within two months!

Only two weeks after the day we were originally planning on transferring with Katie, we had the wedding of our dreams and invited everyone to join us on a wedding celebration cruise. All of our family, friends, and fans were invited to join us. We had a beautiful time, but we also had a lot of time to think. We were sad about the transfer not taking place a few weeks before as planned, but the wedding really helped take our minds off it so we could focus on something else.

Looking out over the ocean was such a beautiful experience. I had a lot of time to think and I knew in my heart that we could no longer move forward with Katie. As much as I had grown to care about her, I no longer trusted her. She wasn't deceitful or manipulative; I simply had lost trust in her and the situation. It didn't feel right. I couldn't go through it again, and I felt giving her another opportunity to do this for us would put me through another experience that I wasn't ready to take a chance on. This was a huge decision. We had no one in line. Our plans to have a baby by the end of the year—and the emotional preparation that went with this—was gone. It felt like a death.

I told deMarco how I felt. He didn't quite understand. He thought I was being a bit dramatic. He was also upset with me in some ways. He felt I was making the decision and as long as she was still willing, we should still work with her. I couldn't really explain it, but I just knew I couldn't. I also sensed that Katie knew she couldn't either.

It was on the cruise that Mary came up to us and said, "I want to talk to you." So, we went into our cabin, and we had a long conversation. There were tears when we told her about our decision to no longer move forward with Katie. She said, "I'm supposed to have your babies." I shot back, "Mary, we know this! But you can't. And if you really feel like you're supposed to, then make it happen." I was so emotionally tired that rather than seeing this beautiful lady sitting in front of me telling me she was supposed to have my babies, after just deciding to no longer work with our current surrogate, I basically yelled at her. Still, she insisted, "I'm serious and I want us to really begin the conversation."

We spent another two hours in that cruise boat cabin talking about every logistic you can imagine. By the end, it all seemed perfect. She had 100 percent coverage with her husband's health insurance because he worked for the post office. She didn't want money but agreed to take a small stipend that we offered. She had gotten pregnant on the pill with her two kids, so she knew she was fertile. Although she had just turned forty years old, the egg wasn't hers, so this was a non-issue. She was a little concerned about her physical condition because she used to have a back issue, and she didn't want it to resurface, but other than that, she really had few concerns. I told her that we had rescheduled the transfer with Katie for July 12. Then I asked her, "Would you be willing to go for your consult with the Reproductive Science Center on that date? I'll just change Katie's ticket to your name." Little did Mary know that she was about to give us the most precious wedding gift, or any gift for that matter. Mary said yes.

6

Our Transfer—Mother Mary

Between the wedding and July 12, a lot happened. When we returned from the cruise, I called Katie and told her that deMarco and I both agreed that we didn't want to wait any longer. After going through all that she had gone through, none of us could know how long it would be before she felt physically, mentally, and emotionally prepared to go through this process again. I also told her that we loved her for being willing to work with us these past months and really tried to assure her that there were no hard feelings. It was a difficult conversation, and I remember exactly where I was when it happened. She cried on the phone and kept saying, "I'm sorry; I'm so sorry." I didn't cry. I had so many mixed emotions. The majority of my frustration was based on finances. I felt like I had given Katie so many opportunities to pull out. Katie explained that when she agreed to do this for us, her life was in such a different place. She didn't know her son would be molested. She didn't know her father would kill himself. Bless her heart, she was right. It was a little overwhelming to think of everything she had been through since agreeing to do this with us. Considering her age and circumstances, I really did feel an enormous amount of love for this young girl. Her intentions were so pure; she truly wanted to make us parents.

Mary obviously had to broach the topic with her husband again. I'll never forget Mary calling me and saying, "I'm going to tell him at dinner tonight." Surprisingly, when she mentioned it this time, her husband was more receptive. He asked more questions and also asked if they would be compensated. Mary explained our agreement, and although we were paying little compared to what most surrogates get paid, every little bit helped. They agreed they could use the extra money to get their daughter braces and pay off a few other small debts. During dinner she ran into the bathroom and called me and said, "He said OK!"

It quickly became so clear that this indeed was supposed to happen. Mary was very spiritual. Rather than being upset with Katie, she told me, I should consider Katie as the angel sent to hold the space for us until Mary was ready to do what she knew from the beginning was hers to do. This helped me tremendously. Katie simply wasn't the right person. Well, she wasn't the right person to have our babies, but she was exactly the right person to hold the space, as Mary put it, to keep our dream alive, to keep the vision moving forward and, ultimately, to bring us to the point of being prepared to move forward with Mary.

I contacted the law firm that had drawn up our contract with Katie and explained the situation. They were amazing and agreed to change the names on the contract to reflect Mary's and her husband's names, and they would not charge us any extra to do this!

The Reproductive Science Center was informed and, although disappointed for us, I think deep down they probably felt, "We told you so!" They had warned us of the very thing that had happened with Katie. But no use looking back. It was all looking forward from here! The staff was already familiar with Mary because when she expressed interest the first time, prior to speaking to her husband, we had told them about her, and she had actually filled out some paperwork. They sent everything else that they needed her to fill out, and they scheduled our consult the day we were going to do the transfer with Katie: July 12. It was all set!

July 12 came quickly. Mary flew to Boston—where we had performed over the weekend—and we picked her up. We had booked so many gigs around our appointments. Fortunately, we were able to work and actually make money on these dates that we would normally be spending so much money. The life of a rock star!

The consult went well, and we talked about everything we had talked about with Katie. It was a little difficult because there were moments I thought, *I can't believe we're here again.* But it was all good. We needed to make sure we were all on the same page. We made it very clear that Mary was like a sister to me, knowing it is very common for sisters to carry children for their brothers, particularly if they are gay. There are some pros and cons. Some doctors prefer a gay couple using someone they don't know in case there are complications with the carrier during childbirth. If a carrier was to have complications or even die in childbirth, it could be extremely difficult for the intended parents if they know her. People could blame them. If she has a family, there could be all kinds of guilt and shame involved. However, on the flip side, knowing the carrier is a blessing because you experience the entire process, strengthening the bond you have with the carrier. Too some it's more personal and feels less like a business transaction.

When all was said and done, we could tell the therapist loved Mary. As long as Mary passed the blood tests, we were good to go. The question was, "When?" When did we want to move forward and transfer?

We talked to Mary. We were ready to do it as soon as possible. Looking at the calendar, we decided fall would be the best. After going back and forth with dates, we landed on September 29, 2010. Dr. Pang was available to do the transfer and the date was set. We would thaw three embryos each on Monday, September 27, leaving three remaining frozen each to use in a future cycle. These would be our backup in case none of the thawed embryos were viable, or if we simply wanted to have more children in the future. Flights were booked, hotel and car reservations were made, and hope was in the air.

The next few weeks were interesting. I had huge trust issues because of what had happened with Katie. Mary continually felt as if I didn't trust her, and it was causing some tension. She kept saying, "You have to trust me!" I was afraid Mary would back out just like the previous surrogates had. It was too good to be true. I didn't want to get my hopes up again only to be defeated. Could I handle this emotionally? What if Mary decided she couldn't do this after all? How would I deal with it? What would we do? There were times I thought, *If she backs out, I'm leaving.* I pictured flying away to another country and starting a new life where no one would know me. I'd be free. Crazy thoughts come to mind when you are emotionally exhausted. I don't think people had a clue I was experiencing any of this. I put on my happy face. Most people didn't even know we were doing this! Isn't it amazing how those we care about may be going through things and we haven't a clue?

Mary started her Lupron shots the last day of August. They were surprisingly easy for her. She was a little hormonal, but I never said that to her. The one thing she had asked of me was that I never suggest she was acting a certain way because she "was hormonal." I had forgotten this and suggested it once, and she was quick to remind me to never say it again. Later, she e-mailed me, "I can't believe I'm going to say this, but I just read about Lupron, and all of my symptoms are related. I think I'm hormonal!" I laughed and thought, *Duh!*

Mary handled the Lupron well. When it came time to take her last shot, she said she actually felt sad. She had a little ritual every night before going to bed. When she did her last shot, she realized this would also be the last night of the ritual. I loved that.

Let's just say the Lupron was much easier than the progesterone. The progesterone needle was quite large, and she couldn't give it to herself. The Universe provided the perfect opportunity when Mary shared with her daughter's Girl Scout leader what she was doing. The leader's daughter and Mary's daughter were friends, and the leader was a nurse for an OB-GYN. "I'll give you your shots," the leader told her. Mary explained they would need to be given every day for eight to ten weeks. The Girl Scout leader said no problem, and so it was. Fortunately, they lived only five minutes away from one another, and Mary would stop by every afternoon to get her shot.

September flew by, and before we knew it we were back in Boston, not even two months after our consult, getting pregnant! We were here. The time had finally arrived! We flew in Monday, September 27, the day of the thaw. We would find out first thing Tuesday morning how many embryos survived the thaw. Again, we were thawing three embryos each. Depending on how the embryos thawed, we would either do a two-day transfer on Tuesday or a three-day transfer on Wednesday. The goal was to do a three-day transfer because this gave the zygotes time to divide and a better chance of implantation.

Dr. Pang also explained that he would not be at our location on Tuesday, so we were really hoping for the third day because we really felt he was supposed to be the one to do the transfer. So, using our spiritual principles, we saw our transfer being on Wednesday, and we envisioned the little zygotes dividing, one of each.

We had continually discussed how many we were going to be able to transfer. Mary was convinced it was going to be twins. She felt so strongly about this that we agreed that even if two of only one of us survived the thaw, we would take our chances and transfer both. Hence, we could have twins from the same father. However, if we had two and only transferred one and that didn't take, we all felt we had gone through too much to not take that chance.

On Tuesday morning, as I lay in bed with deMarco, we received the call. It was Dr. Pang himself—again, unusual that he would call us, but he did. He said we had a decision to make. He explained that out of my three zygotes, only one survived, but it was a four-cell. They usually want to transfer a six- to eight-cell blast. He then explained that all three of deMarco's survived, but they were all only at a two-cell blast. He said that we could either transfer my four-cell blast and choose one of deMarco's, or we could wait overnight and see which of deMarco's continues to divide and hope that mine would survive overnight. If mine did not survive, I would have no embryo to transfer.

deMarco and I looked at each other. I asked what percentage chance there was that my embryo would not survive and, although it was very low, it was still a chance. The chance that none of deMarco's would survive was almost zero. We had come too far and everything had gone too right to rush this, so we agreed that we wanted to wait. Let's just say that that was one of the longest days of my life! The nurse called to schedule the transfer for Wednesday. We were to arrive at 1:00 p.m.

The next morning, I was hoping for a phone call but didn't receive any. I figured no news was good news, but I also wondered what the status was of the embryos. I finally couldn't take it anymore, and I e-mailed Dr. Pang. I simply said, "I am hoping no news is good news." His response was, "You are correct—see you soon."

What a relief! Thank God! When we arrived at the clinic, Dr. Pang explained that my embryo had moved to a seven-cell, and one of deMarco's was a four-cell, one a five-cell, and one an eight-cell, obviously the one they would transfer. So, we had our two—one of each and they would both be transferred in a matter of one hour. We were ecstatic. At least this way we could say it was an even opportunity! Had only one of us had an embryo, I think the journey would have been just as important, but it would have been different. deMarco and I had been through so much together, touring and spending the majority of our nine years together. This was yet another experience we got to share. It was awesome.

The doctor asked if we were going to watch the transfer. We were surprised and didn't even know this was a possibility. We told Mary and she said, "Absolutely not!" I was a bit surprised, but I knew Mary was extremely shy and private. The thought of us in a room with her legs spread wide open did not appeal to her. I explained why this was important to us and practically begged her to let us come in. We were sitting with her in the prep room, and she had to drink a ton of water. She kept feeling like she was going to throw up, so she wasn't very happy. All of a sudden, Mary stopped and looked at us and smiled. "What?" I asked. And she said, "Listen." They were playing "Mother Mary" over the stereo system. She let her guard down, and I promised we'd stay at her head, and we also reassured her that we'd let her get situated first and that we would wait to come in until right before the procedure. She hesitantly agreed. I'm so glad we did!

From that moment, all went so quickly. They took Mary into the room to transfer. It's a basic chair but Mary liked it because you don't put your feet up in anything; instead, it's your knees. I don't really know the difference, but she said it was much more comfortable. She was covered, and we stood beside her facing down toward her feet. deMarco held her hand, and I watched the TV monitor closely. Everything was being shown on the monitor. The doctor was in position with two nurses. He had Mary sign a paper stating that she understood that by transferring two embryos, she may have twins. She stated that she was aware, and she signed it. He took the instrument that would have the embryos in it and did a "test run." Basically, he inserted it through her cervix into her uterus and marked on the monitor where he would reinsert it when transferring the actual embryos. It was a bit uncomfortable for Mary, but she did great. The nurses were extremely encouraging. Then, another nurse came in with a tube. Inside the tube were the embryos. They had taken a picture of the embryos prior to bringing them in, and the picture was displayed on the monitor. We were looking at our little zygotes! I'm not sure exactly how it worked, but the doctor took the tube with the embryos, sucked them into the instrument to insert into Mary, and the next thing we saw was the instrument on the monitor inside the uterus. When he released the first embryo, he explained that they're in an air bubble, and you can actually see the bubble on the screen. We saw the second bubble pop out on the black and white screen, and the doctor said, "Perfect." Could it be that in those short seconds our lives would never be the same? Only time would tell—ten days to be exact. We would find out on Monday, October 11, 2010, whether or not we were pregnant when Mary would go for an official blood test.

I walked out of that office that day feeling a huge sense of relief, yet also feeling like it was still all a dream. It was done. Mary had done her part. We had never gotten this far. It was a beautiful day, and we decided to go do what we all love doing the most: eat!

7

Our Results—Two Sacs

DeMarco and I had planned a trip to Europe. We left on October 4, and although we felt a little strange knowing we wouldn't be here for the pregnancy results, we were glad to get away and be preoccupied until then. We went to Copenhagen, the Netherlands, France, and London. While in Copenhagen, I chatted with Mary on Gmail. She said she'd taken a home pregnancy test that read negative. The next day, she took two more. One read positive and one read negative. I couldn't help but feel like we were being teased. I told her to go and get two more. She did two more and, sure enough, one came back negative and one positive. It was crazy. She said it was rare to get a false positive and was much more common to get a false negative. We were really hopeful, but we still wanted the official blood test.

It was in London on October 11 that we finally got the phone call. I had given Mary our hotel room phone number. deMarco and I had gone and tried to have a nice dinner, but I was so preoccupied. I just wanted to get back to the room in case she called. When she finally called, I said, "So?" She said, "You're going to be a daddy!" We all laughed, and deMarco and I hugged. We had a friend in London who had just come in when I found out, so we told him and we all hugged. I talked with Mary a few more minutes, and then we went out for a gay night in London. All I could think the entire time was, *We're going to have a baby.* I felt so distant from everyone that night. I was in my own little world. All of the work, the time, the heartache, the dreams—and I was finally going to be a dad. We returned to the United States the next morning. I was so happy to land.

After a few weeks of the progesterone shots, Mary began getting a rash. Although the shots can produce lumps, they shouldn't cause a breakout. It itched as well. The doctor switched her to another shot with a different oil, but it only got worse. Finally, after eight weeks, the doctor suggested Mary take suppositories. Believe it or not, this made Mary extremely happy! No more having to get shots, and no more having to go to her friend's house every day. Rather than taking one shot per day, she had to do a suppository in the morning and evening. She'd had her hCG levels (a hormone produced during pregnancy) and progesterone levels checked, and all looked great. The numbers were actually high. We all wondered if it could mean *twins*?

During this time, so many questions ran through our minds. None of them mattered because the most important thing we already knew: we were pregnant. But what if both took? What if both took and then one split? We could have four babies if both took and both split into identical twins. Is it rare? Yes. But is it possible? *Yes!* We would find out on November 1, 2010, how many babies were in there. We couldn't wait!

November 1 rolled around quickly, and before we knew it we were sitting in the OB's office. Mary's levels were still looking good so, hopefully, she would be able to stop the progesterone on November 20 if her level was 20+. This would indicate her body had begun releasing progesterone on its own. Because the eggs were not hers, Mary's body wouldn't begin producing progesterone immediately, and the embryos require progesterone for the implantation and growing process. We learned that many miscarriages with surrogates occur during the first weeks of pregnancy due to the lack of progesterone. However, once a surrogates body realizes it's pregnant, it eventually begins releasing it's own progesterone and the surrogate can stop the progesterone shots, or in Mary's case, the suppositories. I find this quite amazing.

So, things were moving along, and we were in the office about to find out "how many." Mary went back first and got in position, and then they called us back. As soon as the doctor began the ultrasound, she said, "There's two!" Then, when she looked closer she said, "And there are two heartbeats." She continued the ultrasound and everything looked normal. She confirmed they were fraternal as each had its own amniotic sac. *Two! One each!* It was a miracle.

We just looked at each other, and I hugged deMarco. Mary said, "There's only two, right?" We all froze. The doctor confirmed, "Yes, there are only two."

It was hard to see anything clearly on the ultrasound, but we could definitely see the flashing of two little heartbeats on the screen. The heartbeats! We were only six weeks! This experience personally altered my view on abortion. I say this with no judgment, and I consider myself a liberal person. I also believe that no one can truly understand what someone is going through or has gone through unless you have walked in his or her shoes, but how someone can say the little being inside a woman is not alive when you see a heartbeat is beyond me. To me, that is life. It was for us.

I immediately called my parents and told them, "It's twins!" My mom said, "Praise the Lord!"

Now we would wait to find out the next surprise: the genders! Mary was convinced it was a boy and a girl. I had a gut feeling it was two boys. So, we decided to make a bet. We never said what we won, but we were having fun. Obviously, twins were a higher-risk pregnancy. We looked at the due date of June 17, and the doctor said as much as she believes in natural births, a C-section would definitely be safest for Mary and the babies. With twins they would be full term at thirty-six weeks rather than a forty-week gestational period for a singleton pregnancy, so, she gave us the week of May 23 as our option. This was an entire huge decision on its own. Perhaps the twins would come sooner. Perhaps they'd hold off. I had prepared for the babies coming in June mentally and oddly was a bit disappointed they'd have a May birthday. Regardless, we were pregnant, and with twins, one each, biological siblings through Lexi, the birth mother. Magical.

8

Our Pregnancy—Enjoy the Ride!

The pregnancy started out a little bumpy. We had our genetic testing appointment on December 13. Everything had been going fairly well, except Mary had a lot of morning sickness and was not feeling well overall. Being friends with the surrogate has its advantages in so many ways, but it also definitely comes with its challenges. I wanted the pregnancy to be a beautiful experience. I wanted to cherish each step and each moment. However, it was very difficult to enjoy it when Mary was always feeling sick and exhausted. This affected her in many ways, not to mention her being hormonal because of being pregnant, and trying to be there for her was exhausting. I felt guilty and responsible and, at times, thought, *It would be so much easier if the surrogate just lived somewhere else and I wasn't having to go through all of this with her.* Being my surrogate's friend was often difficult for me. She was used to coming to me for support, and as the intended parent I was directly connected to this situation—and the reason she needed support to begin with. Every little thing she felt or complained about caused me to fear, as I thought something might be wrong. Living in that fear was unhealthy, and I couldn't balance my own experience with being there for her.

On December 13, at the genetic testing, the ultrasound technician took a lot of time looking at the babies. It was really cool. We were able to watch everything on a huge flat screen. They had gotten so big! We could see little hands and feet. When the technician first looked, she said, "There's only one placenta." Immediately I knew what this could mean. I had researched enough to know that although many identical twins are in the same amniotic sac, some have their own sacs, sharing one placenta. All along our doctor had been telling us it was fraternal twins, meaning we would have one biological child each. What if? What if only one of our embryos took, split, and these were identical twins? The next shocker—without asking us whether or not we wanted to know—was when she said, "Baby A is a boy!" I have to admit I was excited to hear this. However, when she got to Baby B, and she said, "I think it's another boy!" several emotions went through me. My intuition all along had told me it was going to be two boys and this was now confirmation. I also was happy I had won the bet! However, I felt even more uncertain because if they were both boys, and there was only one placenta, there was a much greater chance that these could be identical twins.

We all were processing a lot in that room. deMarco was somewhat shocked. I think he was so sure it was a boy and girl because Mary was so sure. Even Mary couldn't believe it. I was thrilled with two boys, but I wasn't quite prepared to find out they were identical, mainly because we both thought we were having a biological child at the same time. This may seem irrelevant to some people, as most would think we'd just be thrilled to be pregnant, but after going through so many scenarios, having to make so many intricate decisions, and thinking everything had worked out exactly as we had hoped for, the thought of finding out differently would be an adjustment. One of us would have two biological children rather than each of us experiencing this together.

Fortunately, our OB-GYN's office was in the same building as the genetic testing office, so I ran up to our doctor and asked to see her. I went in and shared what had just happened downstairs. I felt like saying, "But you said it was one of each!" Although I didn't, I'm sure she sensed what I was feeling. She was really sweet and said, "Jason, I'd be really surprised if these are identical twins." She explained that quite often the placentas are pushed together, and it's hard to differentiate between them. She felt confident that they were fraternal. Not only was I nervous about the babies being identical for obvious reasons, but I also knew identical twins were much higher risk. Knowing that they were fraternal would help put our minds at ease for medical reasons as well. I showed her the ultrasound pictures, and she agreed that it looked like two boys. I thanked her for her time and went back down three floors to the genetic testing, feeling a little crazy.

When I walked back in to the examining room, the technician was finishing the ultrasound with Mary. Right before she finished, she said, "Oh, I think I see the membrane." This was the membrane separating the two placentas and the technician agreed that they were probably fraternal and not identical. I breathed a huge sigh of relief, and that was that.

The holidays were just around the corner. We also just entered our second trimester. Time had flown! My parents came to town, and my mom went to an ultrasound appointment on December 17 with Mary and me. It was fun to have my mom there, seeing the babies and meeting our doctor.

On December 21, deMarco and I had just sat down to watch "Brothers & Sisters" after a long day. Then Mary called. "Don't freak out," she said in a shaky voice, "but I need you to meet me at the hospital. I'm bleeding badly." I was immediately reminded of how quickly your life can change in a matter of seconds. I could tell she was scared, and I told her we were on our way. I said to her, "Mary, it's OK. We know it's OK." She began crying and said, "But it's ALOT of blood."

deMarco and I got dressed and rushed out. We arrived at the hospital around 8:15 p.m. It was the emergency care center of the women's hospital. Mary signed in. She had driven by herself. I was a bit surprised, worried, and frustrated that she drove herself in her condition. They took her immediately, but when deMarco and I started to go back, the nurse said, "Only one of you can come." Mary replied, "Nuh-uh." (I appreciate her so much for being so protective and adamant that we were both present for everything during the pregnancy.) Unfortunately, in the case, the nurse said, "It's policy." deMarco said he would wait in the waiting room, so I walked into the room with Mary. I realized they would be doing a lot of internal exams, and with my nervous energy I decided that it would probably be best for me not to stay, so I went back out to the waiting room with deMarco. I told Mary that if they did an ultrasound, I would go back with her. As much as I couldn't even imagine, if something had happened, I didn't want her to be alone when finding out.

That night felt like forever. We sat and waited. I kept thinking, *There is no way anything would happen after all of this.* Every different kind of thought raced through my mind. My stomach was in knots. My head hurt. I felt so bad for Mary. I didn't want her to have to go through this. deMarco was handling it quite well and seemed calm. He helped ground me, but I was a nervous wreck. I kept watching the nurse station hoping to see any reactions. I soon saw the doctor walk in to Mary's room through the glass door. I just kept saying, "God, please, let the babies be OK."

I looked at my phone and a text message had popped up on the screen that I had sent earlier in the day to my brother saying, "It's all good; no worries." I felt a peace at my own words and just started saying that over and over in my head. I suddenly felt calm and at peace and had a knowing that the babies were OK but that the doctor was probably going to put Mary on bed rest. It was so early. We were just over three months with five or six to go.

The nurse came out and said we could come back and that the doctor wanted to see us. It was almost 10:00 p.m. at this point, and mentally I was exhausted. When we walked in, the first thing Mary said was, "The babies are OK." deMarco and I felt like we could breathe again. Mary explained they did an ultrasound, and the babies were kicking and moving. "They have no clue anything is even happening," she said. I was so relieved. I was surprised Mary didn't ask me to go back with her for the ultrasound as we had discussed, but just as I didn't want her to be alone if finding out something had happened, I don't think she felt she could handle watching me find out if something had. Again, I think she was trying to protect me in the midst of her own experience.

The doctor came in and explained that Mary's placenta was low lying, and she had a partial placenta previa. This is when part of the placenta is covering the cervix. Apparently, it causes bleeding if agitated. In Mary's case, actual pieces of the placenta were discharging, making her fear she was miscarrying. Mary said she had done too much the day before: lifting, moving tables, and so on. The doctor told her she should go on bed rest for a week and then go see her OB-GYN for a follow-up. A week! And over Christmas! She had so much to do for her job at the church. She had her own family and their holiday plans, and she had even planned on joining us for Christmas dinner. She was upset, but all we could do was tell her that we loved her and that it was going to be OK. Most of all, we were all so grateful the babies were fine.

Placenta previa happens in about one out of every two hundred pregnancies. Usually, 95 percent of the time when it happens early on in pregnancy, it corrects itself. As the uterus grows, the placenta pulls back from the cervix. So, it would be a waiting game.

deMarco and I had a full schedule the entire holiday and would be out of town at our cabin in the country with my parents. We were having Christmas dinner at our place in the country and staying there through New Year's. It was hard leaving, but we didn't have much choice. And with Mary on bed rest, there wasn't much we could do.

In addition to being on bed rest, Mary got sick. She was vomiting, had a sinus infection, and all of this while bleeding. Her throwing up would cause her to bleed due to the pressure. Her sneezing and coughing didn't help the bleeding stop either. We had so much going on with us that I had a hard time dealing with knowing what she was going through. All the time I was trying to be present with our guests and our duties. The holidays are very important to me and I was frustrated that I wasn't enjoying them due to worrying about Mary.

In the end we made it through. It was probably one of the worst holidays for Mary and her children. Mary's husband helped keep the kids occupied, but it was a rough Christmas for them I'm sure. I felt that Mary resented us. She probably thought it was unfair that we weren't experiencing any of this with her, yet emotionally I felt as if I was on the same roller coaster. It wasn't easy. I just had to remind myself to feel compassion for this amazing woman who was going through this for us. In my frustration, I kept reminding myself of this miracle, and it pulled me through.

Mary went to her OB after being on bed rest for a week, and the OB told her that she thought it would be OK for her to go back to work and do very light activity. After being back at work for about a week, Mary was still spotting, although very lightly.

We visited the high-risk doctor on January 6, 2011, and were able to see the 3D ultrasound. It was neat! The babies don't look quite like babies facially, but we saw their toes, their fingers, their arms and legs, and it was remarkable. The doctor confirmed that everything looked great as far as the babies were concerned. He asked if we were "sure" these were fraternal. I got a lump in my throat and told him we were at first, but at the last genetic testing the technician thought there was only one placenta, until the end when she thought she saw the membrane dividing them. He spent some time looking closer, and he confirmed that he thought they were fraternal, 95 percent sure. He also confirmed they were both boys! Mary still wasn't convinced, but when he pointed out the penis of both babies, it was hard to deny. The doctor also confirmed that one of the placentas was a low-lying placenta, and he asked her if she was still bleeding. She explained that it was very little. He advised her to go on bed rest until she had two full days of no bleeding. This wasn't what any of us wanted to hear, but I knew we should listen to the doctor.

We talked more about it. Mary asked if we wanted her on bed rest. I told her that I wanted to do what was best for her and the babies. She went into work and talked to the executive director of the church and asked if she could take the following week off work. The executive director said, "Go home now. These babies are the priority." That was pretty wonderful.

I have to acknowledge the church community that we worked for. Our surrogate was the youth director at the church. We were involved with the church musically and worked with the youth and young adults. When Mary felt called to do this for us after our wedding, she went to the leadership to let them know her thoughts. Of course, we didn't know if she would definitely get pregnant. We didn't know it would be twins. We didn't know it would be high risk. However, through the entire experience, the church was so supportive of this decision, and I am so grateful that we had their support from the beginning.

Mary went home, and we would wait for two days of no bleeding. In the meantime, deMarco and I had a lot of work to do. We moved our office out of the nursery to our downstairs. I painted the nursery. We unpacked some of the items we had been given as gifts and set them up in the nursery. My dad helped me put them together while visiting over the holidays. It was special. We also began touring again, trying to squeeze in as many bookings before the big day—actually, the big month! We would stop traveling at the end of April. Any weekend we weren't contracted at the church, we would be traveling and performing. We had to save up some money for these babies.

It was January 21 that Mary finally stopped bleeding completely. Oh, happy day! She had been on bed rest for about three weeks and was very antsy. It definitely felt as if we had made it over the hump. We were nineteen weeks into the pregnancy (over half way there!).

deMarco and I discussed trading in his Jeep Wrangler for a minivan. It became a bit of a joke. When I first approached him, he was like, "Are you crazy?" But when we really talked about it, we both agreed the Jeep just wouldn't work with two babies. Just trying to get them in and out of the back seat would be crazy, not to mention the safety issues. So, we started searching. We had considered getting another SUV, but a good friend of mine told me, "Whatever you do, get a minivan." The automatic doors, the ease of putting the kids in and out, and the storage space—it all made sense. We just weren't real big minivan fans. After looking at our options, we settled on four models. We liked the Honda Odyssey, the Toyota Sienna, the Volkswagen Routan, and the Mazda 5. The Mazda 5 looked more like a car, but it did have sliding doors. The doors weren't automatic, though, and this was pretty much the entire reason you'd want a minivan in my opinion, so we scratched that one out. It was smaller than a normal minivan as well, but it looked pretty cool.

We decided the Honda Odyssey and Toyota Sienna were too soccer-mom for us, so we went with the Volkswagen Routan. I'd always loved VW. I liked the look, and deMarco loved the drive and the German suspension. We ended up looking around at some used, some pre-owned, and some dealer owned and landed on leasing a brand new 2011 dark red minivan! We decided to call it the "Daddy Mobile." It was fully loaded and for a minivan, really pretty. I had a rear entertainment system where the kids would be able to watch DVDs while we drove (a must!). It didn't have a navigational system, but we used our phones for GPS, so we were OK with that. The doors opened and closed automatically with the remote; the back hatch opened and closed with the remote; and you could open and close everything from inside at the driver's seat. Everything was falling into place, and we were less than four months away from the big day!

As the weeks passed, we were busy traveling. We made sure we were in town for every ultrasound, which happened once per month. At twenty-three weeks, we were able to get a really cool picture of Baby B's face. Baby A was hiding from us. Baby A was the lower baby, who would come first. Baby B was higher and would come second. Seeing the 3D ultrasound picture was surreal. The doctor confirmed that Mary's placenta was no longer covering her cervix, so her previa was gone. One baby was a little smaller than the other, but it wasn't a concern and, again, confirmed these were fraternal.

At twenty-eight weeks, Mary began feeling contractions, but she was pretty sure that they were Braxton Hicks contractions, which are normal and not a concern. However, she was getting them frequently, so she went to the doctor. The doctor was concerned about Mary's blood pressure, which was too high. In addition, there was a small amount of protein in her urine. These were all signs of preeclampsia. Apparently, if a woman has preeclampsia, the only cure is to deliver the babies, which, at twenty-eight weeks, we did not want. And, of course, the only way to keep the blood pressure from spiking was bed rest.

Mary was sent to the hospital for some further tests. Everything came back pretty normal, but the doctor suggested Mary go on partial bed rest, working from home two days a week and going in two days a week. Mary worked a four-day work week, plus Sunday at the church. Again, this was not what Mary wanted to hear, but we all knew she needed to do what was best for her and the babies.

At thirty weeks, with only six weeks to go to be considered full term with twins, the C-section was set for May 27, 2011. We intended to make it full term. Mary was getting over a bad cold and virus, which gave us a little scare, but everything was fine. She said, "If I can make it through this virus without going into labor, I can make it to the end of this pregnancy!"

At our baby shower, we received so many wonderful gifts. I really felt that we were in a great place, and although there was probably no way to truly be prepared, we were as prepared as we could have been. I even had the diapers in the diaper bags! The nursery, decorated with our jungle theme of monkeys, giraffes and lions, looked great. We still had to go through all of the clothes that were given to us and sort them by age and size, but that would be fun. We were reading more baby books than we knew what to do with. I had to keep reminding myself that people have been doing this for centuries, most of whom had nowhere near the support that we had, or the supplies to start with. So, we were in really good shape.

I hoped that Mary would make it through the last few weeks peacefully. She hadn't been sleeping well, and I'm sure as the babies grew she had more discomfort, but she was a trooper.

I asked her to play our CDs at home or while in the car so the babies could hear us sing. I also suggested that she play some of our YouTube videos so they could hear our voices. We didn't have the chance to spend as much intimate time with Mary as I think we would have liked during the pregnancy, but when we were with her, we talked to the babies, sang to them, and always felt them moving.

Over the last few weeks of the pregnancy, things started heading south very quickly. In honoring our surrogate, I don't want to go into too much of her personal life, but as I shared earlier in this story, she and her husband had been co-parenting, living together but in separate rooms, for quite some time and had intentions of getting a divorce. With Mary's blessing, he had begun dating someone else during the pregnancy but the relationship didn't last or end well. He was somewhat devastated and went in to a depression.

One evening Mary called and said her husband had made some threatening statements and she didn't feel safe. She asked if she and the children could stay with us. Of course we said yes. Not only were we concerned about her safety, but she was carrying our babies.

I'll never forget opening our front door and seeing her standing there, almost eight months' pregnant, with her children, looking scared and confused. She didn't hear from her husband for the next twenty-four hours and honestly didn't know if he was dead or alive. Shortly thereafter she received a call from him. He had checked himself into a hospital where he would remain for a few weeks to get well.

Mary was still on partial bed rest. She lived about thirty minutes outside of Houston and had no family in the area. Her husband drove her kids to school, and she picked them up every day. What were we going to do? Fortunately, there were only about three weeks left of the school year. I told Mary that we would do what needed to be done. If that meant deMarco or me driving her kids to school for the next three weeks, then we would do so. It would be about an hour's drive each way, and her kids would have to get up extra early, but it could be done.

Mary's daughter, Maddie, had a friend in Girl Scouts, and her mother ended up being another angel sent our way. Maddie had weekend-stayovers with her friend frequently and her friend had a brother the same age as Mary's son Sam, who also had some neurological differences. When Mary explained to the mother her situation, without going into too much detail—but enough—the mother offered for Mary's son and daughter to stay with her the entire three weeks Mary would be staying with us. She would drive them to school with her kids and pick them up. This was a miracle! Mary spoke to her kids and explained the situation. Both of them were actually pretty excited. Mary also decided that they would come stay with us at our home on the weekends so she would have some quality time with them.

Over the next few weeks, we had a beautiful experience. It was fun coming home every day knowing Mary was there with our babies. It felt like they were energetically being prepared to come into our lives and our home. We were able to take care of Mary, and ultimately know she was safe and taking care of herself. On the weekend, one of us would go pick up her kids, and they would come and stay at our place. It was a bit crowded, but they had fun. Looking back, I am so grateful we had those last few weeks to spend with Mary. We would lie next to her and feel the babies kick, hiccup, and move, and we were able to connect with them in a way that we hadn't and wouldn't have if she weren't staying at our home.

Mary's husband would check in occasionally. Eventually he came out of his depression and he and Mary finalized their divorce and remain on good terms. I'll actually always be grateful to him because his insurance covered 100% of our medical bills throughout the entire pregnancy. Without his insurance I cannot begin to imagine what we would have paid.

Trying to enjoy our experience while watching Mary going through so many challenges wasn't always easy. Sometimes I am still shocked that after going through so much stress, she was able to make it to thirty-six weeks. I truly believe had she not been on bed rest those last three to four weeks, she would have gone into premature labor, so we will always be grateful that she was willing to listen to the doctors, respect our wishes, and do bed rest. It wasn't easy, particularly for someone like Mary who can't stand to be in any one place too long.

At thirty-four weeks, we had another ultrasound. The high-risk doctor explained that Baby A was starting to grow at a disproportionate rate compared to Baby B. In other words, Baby B was eating everything! The doctor explained that if Baby B continued to grow over the next week or two, we should probably deliver. In addition, Mary's blood pressure remained high, so bed rest was of course recommended.

We had set our date at May 27, but at this point we began reconsidering. We wanted to make it to the thirty-six-week mark, and May 23 was exactly thirty-six weeks, so we decided to move up the C-section to Monday, May 23. Mary's doctor thought it was a good idea and, just to be safe, they decided to give Mary a hormone shot that would help the babies' lungs develop a little more quickly in case she went into labor earlier. So, we all felt we were at a safe point, even if the babies came.

Those last few weeks are a blur. We were just waiting, waiting, waiting. Our gay friends had a gayby shower for us—a gay baby shower. It was fun and really our last hurrah before becoming daddies.

My parents flew in on Friday, May 20. And finally, Sunday, May 22, we were a day before the big day. We had a nice dinner with my parents and Mary, except Mary was having contractions, so she lay on the sofa the entire time. We called her doctor and asked if she thought we should come in. Mary did not want to go into natural labor, particularly considering the babies were both breach, and there was no way she was going to deliver these babies naturally. The doctor said to hold off unless the contractions got really bad, and she said she would see us in the morning. The C-section was planned for 2:00 p.m., and she wanted us there by noon.

Mary began feeling better and had a little to eat. We all then went to bed knowing the following day our lives would never be the same.

9

Hello, World at 2:30 p.m.

When we woke up, Mary had already showered and was sitting on the bed in our guest room. I walked in, sat next to her, touched her belly, and asked, "Are you ready?" She just looked at me and smiled. Tears welled in her eyes, and we both hugged. I knew she was probably scared. I also knew that she felt much of her purpose was being pregnant and being our surrogate and she was probably wondering what was next. She would be dealing with her husband, beginning the divorce she now knew was inevitable, getting back to her work and her life, and also managing whatever emotions would come after having the babies—not to mention the physical healing that follows a C-section.

She had asked a friend from Kansas City to come stay with her after the births, and her friend agreed. With her husband no longer living with her, there was no one to help take care of her after the births, so her friend coming in was another blessing. Her friend flew in the morning of the C-section, and we decided that someone would pick up her friend and bring her to the hospital later that evening, along with Mary's kids who were still in school at the time. Mary had told them that I would text to let them know their mama was OK. In the meantime, Mary's friend went to Mary's house, unpacked, and got settled.

We loaded our new minivan with Mary, and my parents followed behind in their vehicle. The drive to the hospital was interesting. We were listening to meditation music and didn't say a lot. As we drove up to the hospital, deMarco pulled out our Flip video camera and began taping. We wanted to document as much of the experience as possible and had done so the entire process, from the transfer until now. Mary wasn't too thrilled to be on camera, but she didn't complain.

We checked in to the labor and delivery station, and they gave us a room. Mary got prepped, and we were allowed to sit with her in her room. A nurse came in and explained how things would unfold. Mary would be taken separately before the procedure to a room where she would be given her epidural. After the epidural, they would have her on the operating table and allow us to come in and watch the procedure, one on each side, standing at Mary's head. The nurse's name was Julie, and she was a sweetheart. In the meantime, they hooked Mary up and were monitoring hers and the babies' heartbeats. Everything sounded great. In minutes we would no longer have to listen to heartbeats through a monitor. We'd be able to actually feel them beating against us as we held our newborn sons.

We were upgrading to a suite for Mary, rather than a standard hospital room, so I went ahead and settled up with the billing desk so the suite would be ready immediately following the delivery. deMarco and I would also be able to sleep in the suite on a queen pullout bed. We thought it would be nice for all of us to be together. By this time, several friends had arrived who wanted to be there for the delivery, so they were also able to wait in the suite. I told them I would text once the babies were delivered; they could come down to a viewing area where they would be wheeling out the babies for family and friends to view right before taking them up to the nursery station. Everyone was excited, and having them there definitely brought some peace to the situation.

When I came back to the prep room, it was about 2:00 p.m., and we were getting a bit antsy. Finally, the nurse came in and said they were ready. She gave deMarco and me gowns to wear and put us in a waiting room while they gave Mary the epidural and had her prepped for surgery. We had researched and knew the C-section happened fairly quickly once they started. We realized this was really happening; we were about to meet our babies!

Within minutes the nurse came out of the operating room and told us to hurry. We both rushed with her into the delivery room. We could tell something wasn't right. We were quickly shown where to stand, and deMarco whipped out the video camera. The nurse went on to explain that when they gave Mary the epidural, her blood pressure fell drastically, and the babies' began to do the same, so they rushed into emergency delivery. Mary had passed out, and when we got to our position she was just coming to. She was confused, and tears began falling down her cheeks. We held her hands and told her everything was OK.

In those seconds, we heard the first cry, and when we looked up Baby A was already out, and they were rushing him off. They turned him to us on the way out, and before we knew it we heard a second cry. Baby B was out! It happened so fast that we didn't even realize what had happened. We were able to see Baby B come out, and it was incredible. They yelled "Time of birth, 2:30!" I said, "For both?" and they replied, "Yes." They rushed both babies off to a separate room, the NICU station, where they quickly took us.

I will remember the moment for the rest of my life. Both babies were lying on their little tray beds. Both were crying, moving, looking, and experiencing this crazy place we call Earth for the very first time! The nurses asked us their names, and we didn't even know! I said, "The one with the lighter hair is Noah." For some reason, we just expected one to have lighter hair than the other, but in fact, both had pretty much the same color hair, and it didn't look very light at the time. It was a light-brownish color and when wet looked even darker.

We had already been calling the babies by their names in the womb. We had called Baby A "Noah" and Baby B "Mason," so this is what we stuck with. deMarco and I both walked to a different baby and then switched. The nurses were stamping their feet on the birth certificates, but they also stamped our cap and gowns that we were wearing. They wrote the birth weight, time of birth, and length. It truly seemed like we were in a dream. The babies looked beautiful. Noah was four pounds nine ounces, and Mason was five pounds six ounces. We were able to hold the boys, and then we were able to take them in to see Mary who was being stitched up. When we walked in, she looked so much better. Her coloring was back, and she was alert. We put the babies next to her and have a wonderful picture from this moment. We took some pictures and some video, and then the nurses put the babies in their individual plastic cart, and we walked out to the viewing area. I had texted my parents letting them know the boys were here, and when we walked out to the viewing area everyone was waiting. They all looked in disbelief, and we hugged everyone. I was still shaken up by what had happened in the delivery room. There is a moment when every possibility runs through your head. Was Mary going to be OK? What if something happened to her? I'd never even imagined this. Were the babies OK? Surely we hadn't made it this far for something to go wrong. We had imagined this easy experience of walking into the delivery room, talking Mary through the process, and their holding up each baby for us to see while we snapped photos and treasured each and every moment. Instead, it was a whirlwind of panicked and urgent energy where the moments turned to seconds. Yet, here we were, all OK. We made it.

10

Home Sweet Home

Mary was taken to a recovery room where she was closely monitored. deMarco sat with her while I checked in with the family. When I came back, deMarco and I sat with Mary for a bit and talked about what had happened. She was upset that she passed out. She said she had missed the entire experience of giving birth. One moment she was pregnant and getting a needle, and the next the babies were out and they were sewing her up, us and the babies gone. We explained what had happened, and she was just grateful the babies were both OK.

The babies had been taken to NICU. Any babies under six pounds, the staff explained, were taken to the NICU for six hours for observation. If all looked good, they would be able to come down to our suite. The nurse came in and told us that they were ready to take Mary to her suite and asked if we would like to go to the NICU to be with the boys. I'll never forget the walk to NICU. I'm sure I was in a state of shock, but I felt so overwhelmed with love. I was surprised when I realized it wasn't love for the babies I was experiencing, but love and appreciation for Mary. This lady had gone through so much to give us these gifts. The thought of losing her, or something happening to her in the midst of her selflessness, was unbearable. The amount of gratitude and love I felt for this soul was simply beautiful, and I hope I never forget the energy I was walking in as I felt this and stepped off the elevator. Tears fell from my eyes, and I believe that I experienced gratitude in its purest form in that moment.

We walked into NICU, and we had to sign in, wash our hands, and then we were taken over to our beautiful boys. They were lying under heat lamps and simply looked perfect. Mason's breathing was shallow and faster than they wanted it to be, so they were closely monitoring him. It was strange because with Noah being smaller, we had thought if either of them would have any issues, it would probably be him. However, the nurses explained that usually the smaller of twins tends to be the stronger. I guess they realize in the womb that they are going to have to be aggressive to get anything! This plays out to this day.

My parents were allowed to come in and visit with us. Just looking at these two little miracles would make anyone know that we were blessed and favored. God's love for us was manifested in the flesh, lying before us as our precious newborn sons. Having my parents present was such a gift that I will never take for granted.

deMarco and I were able to give the boys their first feeding, their first bath, and change their first diaper. The hospital did a great job helping us both feel included and treated us equally as parents. The hard part was leaving NICU. We simply didn't want to, but we also wanted to check in on Mary and see our friends. We had taken several pictures that we planned on showing everyone down in the room.

When all was said and done, everyone left to go home, including my parents who went back to our place. Mary, deMarco, and I were alone at last and, of course, we ordered room service. The nurse said Noah would be coming down to our room to stay overnight with us, but Mason would need to stay in NICU overnight to be monitored due to his breathing still being irregular. They also explained that this was quite normal with C-sections. During a vaginal delivery, most fluid is pushed out of the lungs when moving through the birth canal. With a C-section, the baby isn't pushed through, so sometimes fluid remains in the lungs, causing irregular breathing. They said the lungs usually clear within twenty-four hours, and they expected this to be the case with Mason.

We were a little nervous and sad that Mason had to stay in NICU, but we also welcomed Noah with open arms when they brought him in. It was a little after midnight, and I'll never forget holding him and looking at his little face and piercing eyes. "My son," I kept saying to myself, "My dream."

Needless to say, at every sound and every movement, I jumped up to look at him in his carrier. The nurse would come in every few hours to take his temperature and check him. deMarco had gone to NICU and spent most of the night with Mason. The nurses took some pictures while he was there, and there is a beautiful one of deMarco holding Mason that evening that we will always cherish. He fed him and changed him and then made his way back to our room to get a little sleep. I didn't sleep much at all that night, and morning seemed to arrive as if there was no night at all.

The first thing I did when I woke up was call NICU to see how Mason was doing. The nurse said, "He's ready to come down!" *Yay!* This was awesome news. They brought Mason down, and our family was together. Ironically enough, the sofa bed that was supposed to be a queen ended up not being a sofa bed at all. I had slept on the floor, which was against safety codes, so the hospital gave deMarco and me a completely separate room next to Mary's. This ended up being a really great situation because it allowed Mary to rest while we had a room with the babies, and when visitors came we could bring them to our room.

It was pretty funny, however, when a nurse would come in to check on the babies and see me lying in the hospital bed. They'd look up as if to ask, "And Mrs. Warner, how are you feeling?" only to see a young man lying in the bed with two babies at his feet. There would be a look of total confusion until I explained the situation and that the birth mother was in the next room. Several times we all got a good laugh at this happening.

The next forty-eight hours flew by. The babies were up and down between our room and the nursery. A few times they were taken upstairs because their temperature was a little low, and they needed warming up. They were also getting their shots and other vitals. The pediatrician did a checkup and said everything looked great. Our doctor came and did her checkup and agreed. She said rarely had she seen twins born this size at thirty-six weeks who were as healthy as forty-week-old newborns. She was very surprised and happy to say the least. So, we were given the OK to go home with them. However, Mary still needed to stay one more night, so we decided to wait for her and all leave the hospital together. This meant one more night of room service!

Mary would be going back to her home with her friend and her children, while we would be going back to our home with my parents and our two new precious baby boys. As this time drew nearer, Mary started realizing this journey was about to end. It was very emotional for all of us, and when I would try comforting her, she had problems receiving it. I never had any worries about her mental health and relationship to the babies, but I knew emotionally this was going to be a journey for her. In such a situation, no one knew what to expect. You can't project emotions or how you'll feel in a situation that you have never faced. We just prayed that she would be strong and feel peace.

Mary called our room, crying. She had talked to the doctor and was reconsidering pumping breast milk for us. Mary had wanted to do what was best for the babies, but her milk hadn't let down and the doctor told Mary not to push herself if she didn't really feel up to it. I told Mary it was completely up to her, but I will admit that I was a bit disappointed. We had read the benefits of breast-feeding, particularly premies. I also wanted to respect Mary's decision. A few hours later, she called back and said, "I'm going to pump." Her milk had let down, and she was gorged, so she really wanted to pump. Sure enough, she pumped the first three months for us. Looking back, I also think this was a nice way for us to stay connected. It allowed for a gradual closure rather than everything ending abruptly after going home from the hospital. And the most important factor looking back is that the boy's health benefited from her pumping.

It was Thursday, May 26, when I went down and signed out the babies. I confirmed with the billing office that everything was taken care of and that Mary's insurance card was on file. They confirmed. Little did I know that they had accidentally put everything under my insurance rather than Mary's and this caused a huge issue that took over a year to resolve and resulted in the hospital losing a lot of money. I would encourage anyone going through this process to ONLY give the hospital ONE insurance card, even if they ask for more. This will help avoid any confusion and hopefully save you a lot of time and energy that I had to spend cleaning up their mistake.

When I got back to Mary's room after signing out, she was in the wheelchair, and her friend was visiting with her. Her kids were still in school and had only been able to come by the hospital once to see her. I'm sure they were relieved that she was on her way home. The next day was their last day of school and, finally, things would hopefully get back to normal for them.

On our way out, my dad had pulled our new minivan in front of the hospital. Mary's car was there as well. We helped Mary into her car and waved as they pulled away. I remember seeing her face and somehow feeling this sadness. We had been through so much together. She had just given us the most precious gift while literally allowing herself to be sliced open. It was a bittersweet moment. There was some closure as she drove off. It was finally *our* time with *our* boys in *our* home—just deMarco and me. As much as we adored and appreciated everything Mary had done, there was a sense of freedom now that the boys were here. There was a sigh of relief. We made it. The drive home with the babies was the most careful I had ever been when driving!

11

Our First Weeks

Everyone warns you, from the moment they find out you're pregnant, how your life will change. "Just wait," they say. "Enjoy your sleep now because you won't get any once the babies get here." "I hope you're enjoying your life now because it all ends when the babies arrive." I would often get annoyed when people would say these things. It seemed so negative to me. Did they not understand what we had gone through to get pregnant? Did they know each and every decision we had to make along the way? They had no clue of every meeting, appointment, roadblock, detour, and question of whether or not this was ever going to happen.

Well, here we were! It happened!

When we got home, we gave the boys a little tour of our home, carrying them around in their infant car seats. We then took them upstairs and showed them their room. We then put them in the pack-and-play and lay them side-by-side, having another great picture moment. They were so small, yet swaddled they looked bigger. They were here, in our home—in their home.

The first few weeks, I was still in bliss. I couldn't have cared less about sleep. The babies were fed every three hours. Fortunately, they were both on the same schedule, which also meant that both of us fed one each. For those first few weeks, my parents stayed with us, and we alternated nights. deMarco and I would get up and feed the boys one night, and the next night my parents would feed them so we could sleep all night. Getting a night's sleep, even every other night, made a huge difference and was a true blessing. *Thank you mom and dad!*

I remember my mom and me taking a break to go swimming in our community pool. I said to her, "It's so much easier than I expected! I already know I want more." My mom just smiled. I'm sure she was thinking, "Just wait."

By the third or fourth week, the lack of sleep began to take its toll. The boys were angels. They were on schedule and pretty much ate, pooped, and slept. Mary was pumping, and they were doing well on her milk. However, getting up every three hours was exhausting. My dad had left to go back to Tennessee, and my mom was about to leave. We had started getting up every night to prepare for being on our own. At one point, we considered one of us taking care of the boys one night and then alternating, so we'd each at least get one night of sleep. It never happened. We both continued getting up every night feeding one baby each. It became a bonding experience in many ways, and we enjoyed it in the midst of our delirium.

We were on our own for about six weeks until deMarco's mother came to visit. My mom ended up coming back during this time as well, so we had both our mothers' support again. Again, it was a huge help. During this time, we began getting back to work and trying to come up with a routine for us as well as the babies. We scheduled our workdays and tried to make it fair for everyone. It wasn't always easy. I was trying to get a nonprofit up and running; deMarco was starting a health and wellness business; we had our job at the church working with the youth; and we were contracted to do a few more dates before the end of the year. The biggest two dates we had coming up were a Mary Kay convention in Dallas that was over a three-week period and a Halloween cruise for which we'd be gone a week. Looking back, I can't believe we did it all, but we did.

The Mary Kay gig came at a great time, financially, and as difficult as it was flying back and forth to Dallas and being gone from the babies a day or two at a time, it was a nice break for us. It was also fun. My mom was staying at our home with the boys during that time, and she was a true rock star. Though they were good babies, handling both at the same time wasn't easy for anyone. And by this time they had started experiencing the "witching hour." Around 5:00 p.m., every evening, both boys would begin screaming. No matter what we did, they'd scream for a few hours, and then all of a sudden they would be fine. It was hard when both were experiencing this because you couldn't really give both your full attention if you were alone. Somehow my mom did it. Before we knew it, three weeks were over, and we had money in the bank with several fun memories, and more importantly, several nights of good sleep.

Mary would come over about once per week to see the babies, deliver milk, and pick up empty bottles to use for pumping. It was around the three-month mark when we realized Noah was starting to act very uncomfortable after feedings. Mary put the date on the milk she pumped and I remember asking her what she had eaten on a certain date of pumped milk that I had fed Noah. She went through her diet that day and said that she had eaten fried egg rolls from Jack In the Box on that particular date. I didn't want her to feel guilty, but I told her Noah had a really bad reaction to the milk from that day. It was difficult for Mary. We had asked her to stay away from several things while being pregnant. Now, after her 'job' was done, she was still being told what and what not to eat. She had been so giving, so, we decided we would transition the boys to formula and finally relieve Mary from being so generous of her time and energy—and milk!

We first tried Nature's One organic baby formula, but it seemed to constipate both boys. We then tried Earth's Best organic, and although it worked well for Mason, Noah still had issues. This began the whirlwind of finding the right formula. We tried a formula the hospital had given us, which was Enfamil. He threw that up. We tried regular Similac, and he threw that up. We had one sample of Similac Sensitive and, sure enough, he kept it down and didn't seem to fuss as much after drinking it. We kept him on this for the next three months until we moved him back to Earth's Best at six months. It was so nice to have the boys on the same formula at that point! It would have been much easier to put Mason on the Similac Sensitive as well, but we wanted him to have the organic if at all possible. We probably put ourselves through a lot more work than we needed to in many ways, but we thought we were doing what was best.

At three months, a lot shifted. We were on our own again, with no help from our mothers, and this time for a while. The babies were "waking up," and those first few weeks of sleeping little angels turned into very aware beings who knew how to cry and weren't afraid to do so. The boys were 'good' babies, but a baby's scream is a baby's scream, and you have to learn how to patiently deal with your baby when you are exhausted and worried. When you hear your baby scream, you want to fix whatever is wrong. It's so hard when you can't, or when the baby can't tell you what is wrong. Mentally it can be grueling. There were times my stomach would just be in knots any time I heard the cries. It's a very stressful experience, particularly when you are already exhausted, and all you can do is wait and hope. And pray. I remember one night I held Mason up and looked in his eyes while he was screaming. I spoke to his soul and said, "You are here to teach me. What can I learn from you?" I knew in the midst of everything I was being tested and growing. But let's face it. When you're beyond tired and begging for a few minutes of peace, asking their souls these questions isn't always easy.

Mom and Dad seemed to enjoy Houston on their visits, so I began talking to them about permanently relocating. It was so natural having my mom help with the boys, and after having her, I couldn't imagine having anyone else, particularly those times we had to travel and leave the babies overnight. I could trust my mom, and she adored the boys; they brought her so much joy.

Mom and Dad decided to come back in October and stay through the holidays. If all went well, they said they would be willing to commit to staying a year. During this time, a neighbor two doors down was going through a divorce. When I asked her what she was going to do with her house, she said she was going to let it go into foreclosure.

I was fortunate enough at the time to be taking real estate classes. I'd always enjoyed real estate, and we had purchased a few investment properties over the years, but I was now considering it more seriously as a career opportunity. If nothing else, I felt it would be a way to make some extra income on the side. I had just completed a course when this situation with my neighbor arose, and I thought it would be a great opportunity.

So, my neighbor sold me her house, owner financing it for the amount she owed on the house with no money down. Essentially, I took over her mortgage. I put some money into rehabbing the house, and it turned out beautiful. My parents moved in and lived there for a little over a year before I sold it. It truly was the best thing that could have happened. Some would think having your parents two doors down would be too close, but trust me, they knew as soon as they walked in our door that they would be put to work, so they very much kept to themselves!

12

DADDY'S DISCOVERY

Having children does change everything. I can't imagine my life without them. Every time I look at their faces, I smell their hair, touch their hands, feel their fingers curl around mine, and even when I pull them close and smell their breath, I experience a piece of heaven. They are a daily reminder that I am loved by a GREAT God and that *anything is possible*! Are there hard days? Sure. Are there times I have wondered, *What the heck did we do?* Sure. But one look at them, and there is no question that I would never or could ever imagine a life without them in it. It would feel absolutely empty.

I have a lot of dreams. Most of them seem to fall under the umbrella of SAFE (Safe, Affirming, Family, Environment), the nonprofit I started in 2011 that I haven't shared much about in this book. (You can read more about it at www.safehouseforall.org.) My vision for SAFE is laid out quite clearly, and I do believe it is part of my life's purpose. I have a dream of creating a community that will also be a family to many. This community will provide homes for a lot of children. We will help gays and lesbians become parents through educating them on their options and working with agencies to connect prospective parents with foster children we house in our community.

I don't know if deMarco and I will use our remaining embryos to have another biological child. We were given the miracle of Mason and Noah, one biological each. I think if we have more children, we will help children out there who need a home. Then the question becomes, "What do we do with our leftover embryos?" We spent so much energy creating them. It would be difficult to just let them go. I know time will tell, and eventually we'll know what to do.

For now, every day, I simply sit in awe as I watch Mason and Noah grow. I watch deMarco with them, and I feel like I'm living my fairytale. I treasure each and every "first" experience, whether it's their first word, or their first laugh, or their first potty on the potty. It makes me realize how many firsts there will be—each one passing by until one day we watch them get on the school bus for the first time, then go to prom, then graduate, then get married, and eventually perhaps have their own children, beginning their own journey of parenthood.

I am ever aware of the cycle of life. Somehow on this big Earth, we forget that we are all ONE family. We all need one another. Instead, we often seem to focus on our differences rather than our ONENESS. Many of us come from different places, with different backgrounds, and each his or her story. Yet, most of us experience life in similar ways, with similar emotions. I believe that we are all much more alike than different. We are part of the same tribe: this human race, this ONE human family.

I marvel at the mystery of how one different choice could change everything. If Grandpop hadn't met Grandmom, what would have happened? I wouldn't be me. Looking at Mason and Noah, I think about the fact that on that one day, it was that one sample that had that one sperm out of millions, and it was chosen and inserted into that one egg that could have been one of many over Lexi's life. It brings me to the scripture that I've treasured from the time I was a young boy: "Before you were even formed in the womb, I knew you." Jeremiah 1:5 No doubt there is a great deal of science and brilliance behind ART, IVF and surrogacy, but in the end it still comes down to Divine providence. As much as we would like to think we're in control, we're not.

I'm so grateful Mason and Noah were part of Divine providence and that their souls chose us as their parents. I believe we all choose one another. "Even before we are formed," we know one another and agree to make the journey together. I believe that we are here to live out and fulfill our soul contracts with one another, learning and growing from one another. I'm so grateful I get to travel this journey with Mason and Noah. I look forward to the many lessons I will learn from them. I'll try to never take for granted their laughs, their smiles, their cries, and even their screams. In the most difficult times, I will always try to stop and remember a day when those laughs, those smiles, those cries, and even those screams were the dreams of a young man who wondered once if they would ever come true.

They came true as Mason and Noah.

Careful before you say "Listen to me"

Children will listen

Careful the wish you make

Wishes are children

Into The Woods — Children Will Listen

13

I Fought the Law, and the Law Won

The legal side of our journey was one of the most confusing. I truly felt like I had to educate myself and was ready for the bar when completed, literally and legally.

This will be the hardest part for me to remember because I never truly understood as events were unfolding. Trying to remember the steps, now, is even harder. That's why I asked Richard Vaughn to contribute the next chapter in this book. I feel it's so important for people to understand the steps throughout the entire legal process.

At times I got frustrated because I felt the firm just wanted to tell me what to do and not explain it. Some may be fine just signing on the dotted line and trusting, but I prefer to understand everything. I wanted to know the order in which things would be done and, more importantly, why.

From the onset, we knew that we both would not be able to be listed on the birth certificates. This was very frustrating for me. Having just moved from California to Texas, it was even more difficult because in California they would have allowed both, deMarco and me, to be listed as intended parents on the birth certificate. However, in Texas, only one of us would be able to be considered the "parent," and the other would have to adopt our children! It seemed crazy and still seems crazy. However, the law won.

I remember going to dinner with a wealthy, older gay man who *was* a friend, and I had considered telling him if he financially supported a lawsuit, I would be willing to take this to court in the state of Texas to try and change the law. This was the advocacy side of me coming out and my wanting to stand up for our rights. Our friend wasn't very interested in helping us fight anything. Although he is gay, he is conservative, and he actually had the nerve to say, "Well, the child won't be both of yours. It will only be one of yours." I took this very personal and that was the last time we had dinner with this man.

It was a very sensitive topic. For some reason, it was important to me to be listed on the birth certificate as the "father." Perhaps it's ego, but regardless, it is what it is. It didn't seem fair that we had to choose which of us would be the "father." I talked to deMarco about it, and although he said that he would like to be listed as the "father" as well, it didn't seem quite the issue to him.

Not only would only one of us be listed as the "father," but the surrogate, Mary, we were told would be listed as the "mother." Even though she isn't the biological mother, because she was the one giving birth she would, by default, be listed as the "mother" on the birth certificate. Apparently this is the hospital's procedure and is generated automatically by a computer.

Then, after the births, we would have to actually pay an attorney more money to have Mary's name removed. We were advised that prior to getting the baby's social security number, we would definitely not want Mary's name attached to the birth certificate as this can cause issues later.

In addition, because we both wouldn't be able to be listed on the birth certificate, we'd then have to pay an attorney more money to handle a second-parent adoption. So, after the babies were born, the surrogate would have to be removed as the "birth mother," and deMarco or I would have to adopt, depending who was listed as the "father." We were also told the adoption could take months. So, essentially, as the second parent, you don't have full parental rights of your child until this process is complete.

Interestingly enough, if we had chosen to have the babies in California, we could have gone to court prior to the birth and get a court order that both of us be put on the birth certificate as the intended parents. We considered taking Mary to California the last few weeks of the pregnancy, but if she delivered early, it would disrupt our entire plan. In addition, driving across the country with an eight- to nine-month pregnant woman is probably not the best idea, and she couldn't fly that far into the pregnancy. So, it looked like having the babies in Texas and doing the second-parent adoption was our only option.

The law firm we were working with offered to handle the second-parent adoption for us for $3,000. With twins, they charged double, so it would be $6,000. This was a lot of extra money to simply be listed as our children's parents!

The attorney handling our birth order in Texas, who was working with the firm in Los Angeles as a contractor, also charged $3,000 for a second-parent adoption, but fortunately she charged only $300 for the second child if it were twins. It was a no-brainer that we would use her for our second-parent adoption process.

Knowing we were having fraternal twins, one biological child each, we asked our attorney whether the hospital would allow each of us to claim our biological child as the "father" on the birth certificate, even though they were fraternal twins, and then legally adopt the others? Or, would one of us claim to be the father of both babies, listed as the "father" on both birth certificates, and the other adopt both? Often, it seemed no one could provide a firm answer, and there were several times I simply got a "hmmmmmm?" For us, it all came down to finances, and whichever was the most cost-effective is what we chose to do.

The egg donor contract was by far the easiest. Lexi and Ben basically had to sign a contract saying that they relinquished any legal rights or responsibilities to any birth resulting from the implanting of embryos created from Lexi's eggs.

The surrogate contract was much more involved, and we needed to make sure we were all on the same page and that the financial arrangement was clear. Often a trust is created that pays a surrogate. We decided to just pay her directly. It was a little difficult considering Mary was a friend, as she needed and wanted to be protected and yet didn't want to ask for too much from us. On the other hand, we wanted to offer her the world but were limited in what we were able to do financially.

Fortunately, the law firm handled the paperwork, and it was nice having them as the middleman with Mary and us. I think we ended up just having a heart-to-heart conversation about it before she signed the papers. I reassured her that we would take care of her and that we would do whatever we needed to do. We agreed this wasn't a typical arrangement or agreement and that we were all going to have to trust one another.

Legally, the law firm forces you to examine every possibility. It's good, but it can also cause a lot of anxiety. There are so many factors and things that can go wrong that you don't even consider until you read a contract. It's their job and responsibility to make you aware and help you protect yourself, but it can be overwhelming.

There were several contracts, orders, agreements, disclosures, and so forth, but when all was said and done, deMarco and I were the legal parents of our children. I had to remain focused on the positive—that we actually can be parents. In some states in our country, same-sex couples cannot be listed as legal parents of their children. I think this is criminal. I hope more and more people will realize that children need love, period. There are so many different kinds of families, and when a child has the opportunity to be in a home with loving parents, those parents should have full parental rights concerning that child.

Working with my nonprofit, I have seen the number of children in foster care who are in desperate need of loving parents because their biological parents were more than likely straight, heterosexual people who could not care for their children. Thank God there are gays and lesbians who are desperately trying to foster and adopt these children. Could the Christian right stop their judgment for a moment to really consider the number of children who have been failed by their heterosexual parents and saved by gay or lesbian parents willing, able, and desiring to provide a loving family to them?

Love makes a home. I hope in some small way our family will be a light to many who question, doubt, or even disagree with gays and lesbians having children and that these generous and courageous gays and lesbians who are willing to take on the task and joy of parenting will be honored and respected rather than discriminated against and demonized.

In the end, we've learned that there have been cases in the state of Texas fighting for same-sex parentage on the birth certificate and our attorney believes it's only a matter of time before the courts rule in our favor. Interestingly enough, the hospital knew our situation and chose not to list our surrogate, Mary, on the birth certificates. They only filled in the "father." The "mother" was left blank. If our attorney is correct, and Texas does change the law in the future, we will be able to have our birth certificates amended to have both of our names. It will no longer be "father" and "mother" but "Intended Parent 1" and "Intended Parent 2." I look forward to that day.

14

A Note from Our Surrogate

Jason and I have become very close over the last five years. We say that we are siblings. I'm the sister he never had, and he's the little brother I never had. We are, I feel, soul twins.

It didn't start out that way. I remember first meeting him. The church where I was the youth and family ministry director had hired him and deMarco to be a part of the music ministry team. Jason was also going to be working with me in the youth program. It surprised me that every time I had a meeting with Jason, deMarco always seemed to be there, too.

At our initial meeting I, of course, took note of how strikingly beautiful they were. Jason talked and talked while deMarco hardly said anything but took a ton of notes. I had a strange connection with Jason. I got him right away, but I could also feel what I perceived to be his ego. He wanted to walk into my program, part time, and take over some portion of the youth program. He seemed to focus on what he would be in charge of and his title. Additionally, I had previously reviewed his website, which mentioned their faith background, one that did not align with the beliefs we held at Unity. Frankly, it irritated me. How could he be present only part time, not even believing as we did, and expect to be in charge of anything? What I now know about Jason is that his soul knows way before his head does. His head then spends an endless number of hours trying to figure out what his soul is telling him. Knowing that of him now, I find remembering this funny. You see, his soul knew that we were meant to do good work together. His head just had to figure out how that looked and how it would work.

I was surprised by how quickly we became close. I was also surprised by how much alike we were. We were very similar in many ways. We even looked similar, and countless times people asked if we were related. I always said, "Yes, he's my brother."

Before we knew it, I began working with them supporting their music ministry as well as assisting with the young adult ministry at Unity, in addition to the work we were initially doing within the youth program. I worked for them, and they worked for me.

Jason had shared that they wanted to have children. They had already harvested and their embryos were banked. They now just needed to find a gestational surrogate to carry the baby. I had shared my pregnancy experiences with him, both having challenges. My grandmother had twelve children and loved being pregnant; that did not get passed down to me. I knew that they had been in conversation with a girl at church about it, but she didn't seem like the right one to me. I then had a dream. In that dream I felt like I was being told that I was to be the one to carry their babies for them. Yes, *babies*. In the dream I was shown two, one that had light hair and one that was darker. I thought that I was crazy for even thinking of being their surrogate. My kids were older; I had a job, a family. I was thirty-eight at the time and thought I was too old. And I didn't like being pregnant. What was I thinking? So, I just sat with it.

A while later, Jason and I met up for dinner. All through dinner this dream kept creeping into my thoughts, and I just pushed it aside. Finally, I had to tell him. I told him about the dream, that it was all crazy, but that maybe I was supposed to do this for him. He laughed, as he does, and sweetly dismissed it. *Whew!* I breathed a sigh of relief. I didn't want to be pregnant! The interesting thing, though, is that his head started thinking about it, and he really began to question me about the dream and to analyze it with me.

He then met Kelly at a conference, and they began the process of her being the gestational carrier. When that seemed to be falling apart, Jason came back to me and asked me if I would still consider doing this for them. I said I would. This was a very spiritual experience for me, and there was something at my core that kept prodding me to do this. I knew the obstacle would be my husband. So, we planned to have the guys over for dinner so that he could get to know them better and to discuss the option further. Just prior to the dinner, we had a young adult conference in Houston and I was rooming with a girl named Katie from Dallas. I had become friends with Katie through Facebook. One morning during the conference Katie shared with me that the night before she had a dream that she was having a baby but that it wasn't hers. She also shared that she had always had an interest in and fascination with surrogacy. After sharing this with us, we all felt that if this didn't work out with me, perhaps she would be another option.

So, I had the guys over for dinner, and the end result was that my husband could not let go of the thought of "his wife" carrying another man's baby! So, that was it. Jason and deMarco quickly contacted Katie and began discussions with her. I was devastated. I remember sitting on the church steps and Jason asking me what was wrong. I began to cry and told him that I was sad that I wasn't going to be "the one." He acted as if I should just get over it. I was in mourning, and I think he couldn't go there with me. He had been through so much already that his focus was just on making it happen, and he was also a little angry with me because he felt that I could have swayed my husband if I really wanted to.

So, being friends with Katie, I did my best to support them. Every time there was an "issue," I just kept feeling that of course there were issues because I was "the one"! I was supposed to be doing this, not her.

After a lot of up and downs with Katie, there was Jason and deMarco's wedding, which was probably one of the most amazing nights of my life. It was so incredibly magical and beautiful in so many ways. The next morning we left for the cruise.

The following day Jason found me on the ship, and we sat down to have a heart to heart. He shared his feelings about what was going on with Katie, and I told him that I knew deep down she wasn't the right person to do this. I still felt like it was mine to do. He nodded, and I think he either was too tired to fight it anymore, or he finally got it. We agreed to wait until the cruise was over and we were back home before we sat down with deMarco to discuss the possibility.

The cruise was amazing. Jason had a weird energy, however. I don't think—until now, since reading this book—that I understood why. You see, my soul knowing that Katie wasn't right and that I was "the one" made me not take all of their challenges to heart. Jason, on the other hand, took it all to heart and breathed in every little thing. My heart really goes out to him. He is such a beautiful soul, and all I have ever wanted for him is to find his joy.

On the last day of the cruise, I was anxious. How would we make this work? How would we get my husband to agree? What would deMarco say? I kept telling myself that if this truly was a spiritual experience, if I truly was "the one" who was meant to do this, then everything had to fall into place; it had no other choice. So, Jason and I went to his cabin to have another heart to heart. He, of course, was trying to figure it all out in his head. We talked about ideas, logistics, how it could work. Then deMarco came into the cabin. I was surprised that Jason called him out to the balcony where we were sitting.

deMarco was hard for me to get to know. He was so different from Jason and me. He was quiet. He thought differently. He also had the biggest heart of anyone I knew. He was a soft giant. He would stand and fight for me no matter if I was right or wrong. He was my warrior. So, when he came out to the balcony and Jason started telling him that Katie was done and that we were going to explore my doing it, he turned around and walked back into the cabin. I quickly followed him. He was emotional. This had been a long journey for him, too. I asked him what was going on. He was concerned about starting all over. He also said that he would hate for anything to come between us and damage our relationship. All I could do was reassure him I felt strongly that I was supposed to do this.

The day after we got home from the cruise was the last day of school for my kids. I had to act fast, but how and when would I talk to my husband? How would I get him to agree? My son's friend had asked if he could spend the night that night. So, only my daughter was there, and she was going to a girl scouting event after school. My plan was to take my husband out to dinner and then try to have a heart to heart so he could see why this was important to me. So, I prayed. I prayed to God and my angels. I asked if this was truly mine to do that all would fall perfectly into place and would happen easily. And it did. I had the heart to heart. And he said, "Fine." That was it! It was done. I snuck into the bathroom of the restaurant and called Jason to tell him the news. I couldn't believe it!

The next step was making sure my kids, ages ten and twelve, were OK with it. Being pregnant affected the entire family, not just me. Mommy was going to be pregnant and not as active with them. It was also important the kids understood that these babies were not going to be their siblings and would not be living with us afterward. So, I took the kids over to Jason and deMarco's house one night where we played games and ate pizza. It was really a lot of fun. We also set aside time to talk about what would happen and answer any questions they had, and to get their buy-in.

People have asked how I explained it to my children, and this is what I told them. It's like Jason and deMarco want to make cookies. They have the flour, the milk, and all the ingredients, but their oven doesn't work. So, they asked me if they could borrow my oven to bake the cookies. When the cookies are done, do we get to keep them since they were baked in our oven, or do the cookies belong to Jason and deMarco? The kids said Jason and deMarco.

I then explained that babies start out as little embryos, and they need a warm, safe place to "bake," to grow, until their bodies are done, and then they will be ready to come out. The place to do that is a uterus, and since only women have those, they want to borrow Mommy's uterus to grow their baby until it is ready to come out. Then, it will go home to live with Jason and deMarco, and they will be the baby's daddies. The kids seemed fine with it. My son was a little concerned about my physical well-being, but once we talked through it he was OK. We asked if they had any questions. My daughter said she did but was embarrassed to ask, so she whispered in my ear, "Will you and Jason have to kiss?" How funny! Of course, a ten-year-old thinks that is how babies are made! So, we explained that the embryos are in the freezer, and a doctor will take a long tube to put them in Mommy's uterus, and no kissing would take place!

The next eight months were a blur. Jason recounted much more than I remember. I didn't remember getting the rash and having to go to suppositories until I read his manuscript. I remember the shots, and the blood tests, and getting sick, and even falling one time and having to go to the hospital to make sure the babies were OK. I will say that when you are carrying children belonging to someone else, there is a lot more pressure in doing everything 'right'. Every mother wants to give her baby the best start and do all things right during the pregnancy, but when someone has invested time and money and energy and their future family in your hands, or womb as it may be, it adds pressure.

I think during the pregnancy my relationship with both Jason and deMarco grew and deepened. We often looked at one another as siblings, but now we truly were family.

People have asked me why I became their gestational carrier and if it was a hard decision to make. The answer is, I wouldn't do it for anyone else. I essentially gave up a year of my life for them. There were challenges and tough times, both emotionally and physically, but there were also times that were amazing, like when the babies would be kicking hard, and their daddy would start to sing to them, and they would stop and be still. It was a very intimate experience and not one that I would share with anyone else.

I've also been asked if it was difficult to "give the babies up." My answer is this: How can you give up something that isn't yours? These babies were never my babies. I never worried about parting from them physically once they were born. And, truthfully, that wasn't hard. I miss them when I don't see them, but it is no different than missing those I love when they aren't around.

I felt the difficult part was going to be the separation from Jason and deMarco as well as a bit of "culture shock." Any pregnant mom knows that she is always lavished with attention while pregnant. Once the baby comes, the focus is then shifted, but the mom is there with the baby. For me, I would walk out of that hospital and go home alone, while the guys go home with the babies. I shared this fear with the guys, while making it clear that I knew they would be getting used to being new daddies, and I didn't want to interfere with that. I also made sure I had loving friends to surround me once it was all said and done.

It ended up being a beautiful experience. Because I supplied breast milk for the babies, I would get to go over every two to three days to restock. So, I was able to stay connected during that precious time with the guys and the babies. Over this past year, I've had weekly visits with them to watch them grow and thrive in the love.

Jason and deMarco are incredible dads! They are so natural with the boys, since day one. There is immense love in that household, and those sweet babies adore their daddies. For anyone who may question, or think differently, what I know to be real is love. This house is overflowing with love, and that is all that matters. It is a true honor every time they open their door and welcome me in.

This experience is nothing I will ever forget and something I will always cherish. I adore and love my brothers, and if they asked me again I'm sure I would say yes, though I think my clock has stopped ticking. As far as the babies, I have a very special bond with them. They are my godsons. I love seeing them as often as I can, and oh they make me laugh and smile and are so beautifully amazing. Just as no one can love you like your mother, while I am not their mother, we have a special bond that no one else on the planet will ever have.

15

A Note from Mom Mom

Children are a blessing from the Lord.

"Lo, children are a heritage of the Lord and the fruit of the womb as His reward. As arrows are in the hand of a mighty man, so are children of the youth. Happy is the man that hath his quiver full of them. They shall not be ashamed they shall speak with the enemies in the gate" (Psalm 127:3–5).

We are so thankful for our three sons, Robert Jason, Vance Gerald, and Chad Stuart, and their partners in life, deMarco, Kelly, and Heather. We are so grateful for all of our grandchildren!

When my husband, Bob, and I learned that Jason would not fulfill our dreams for him to have a wife and family, we were heartbroken. I grieved for at least two years. Then, I knew I needed to release our son and watch how God was going to use this situation and our lives to work for good. I decided to trust.

Since letting go, we have been so blessed. We have gotten to know and love so many people in the GLBTQ community, many who are reconciling their spiritual lives and sexual identities. I will never forget finding myself, a born again, spirit-filled Christian woman, sitting in a Metropolitan Community Church (MCC) surrounded mostly by GLBT people in the congregation. I quietly sat there and asked the Lord how I should react to all of these people, and all God spoke to my heart was, "Love them. Show them My love." This is where I believe the church has failed mostly, walking in love and grace, not only with the GLBT community, but with *all* people.

To be honest, when Jason told us about his and deMarco's plans to have children, I had very mixed emotions. I was very close to my mother growing up. I thought, *How can you bring children into the world without one of their parents, a mother or a father, but especially a mother?* Yet, many children aren't being raised by a mother, whether due to divorce, being raised by widows or widowers, some foster children being raised by a single father or mother, and some orphans who have no parents and are being raised by a community. What I have always believed is that the most important thing is to be in a family that loves you. God is love, and as long as we are loved and walk in His love, God is present.

When we finally found out that Mary was pregnant after the fertilized eggs were implanted, we were so excited! Then, we were doubly excited that she was going to have fraternal twins! We could hardly believe the blessing to each partner, having his own biological child as well as a love child of the other to welcome into our family. It was truly a miracle.

We prayed hard for a safe pregnancy and delivery for Mary and the babies. I remember praying most of the nights and days over the Christmas holiday when Mary was bleeding that she and the babies would be OK. My grandmother on my mother's side had lost a set of twins at birth, and my cousin had also lost a set of twins. I prayed that God would bring restoration to our family. God not only answered my prayers with Mason and Noah, but that same year Jason's brother called me on my birthday and told us that he and his wife were also having twins, a boy and a girl! How exciting and wonderful to have two sets of twins in our family in one year—Jason and deMarco's in May of 2011 and Jason's brother's in October of 2011. We will be eternally grateful to Mary, the surrogate, as well as to Lexi, the donor, and her husband for their gift to us and our entire family. It took a village.

We are so grateful that all went well with the births and the babies. We stayed and helped Jason and deMarco with Mason and Noah and what an exciting time in all of our lives. Every day was and continues to be a new adventure as we learn to care for twins. Jason and deMarco always express their gratitude, and we are so happy to be a part of their lives. Every day is a beautiful memory, full of feeding, bathing, and dressing two beautiful baby boys.

We moved to Houston shortly after the boys were born, helping as much as possible, which allowed Jason and deMarco to continue their music ministry.

Although difficult at times, we enjoy touring with them and look forward to the new experiences this will bring. As a grandmother, I realize that in many ways I am able to fulfill a maternal role in Mason's and Noah's lives, and I do feel a sense of responsibility to them. In return, I am reminded daily that they are actually two angels sent to me from heaven.

I love you, Lord. You are so faithful. So true. So beautiful. So wonderful. How can I ever thank you enough for all of the blessings of love in my life? And, now, a double portion blessing: Noah Avery and Mason Alexander.

Epilogue

Interestingly enough, after years of feeling emptiness and a lack of joy, I thought Mason and Noah would be my ultimate joy. What I discovered is that no one, or no thing, can ever be your ultimate joy, not even your children. Ultimate joy comes from within. It's funny because I've known this for years, and I've heard so many teachers share this truth. It's no different from love. Many of us have heard or read that until we love ourselves, we cannot love another.

I feel it so deeply, but it's hard to articulate. When I use the word *possibility*, you can also substitute this with *dream*. However, the word *possibility* feels right to me.

There is no question that Mason and Noah are the joy of my life, but they aren't my ultimate joy. Without them, I would have never fully understood this; not that I fully understand it now, but it's definitely much clearer. I've realized that joy cannot be based on any one external experience. Joy is a journey, just as the surrogacy was a journey, and just as life is a journey.

My ultimate joy and profound discovery that I made is that *anything is possible*. Dreams do *still* come true. Mason and Noah symbolize my possibility of possibilities, my miracle of all miracles, my dream of all dreams. I now have an understanding that when we truly believe in a possibility, and feel it in the depth of our soul, and then put action behind it, we have the potential to manifest *anything. Anything!* We were able to cocreate the possibility of life and watch it manifest. It's truly breathtaking.

Mason and Noah, by far, are the largest possibility of my life. And that possibility manifested on May 23 of 2011. If the largest possibility of my life has manifested, then I know that any other possibility has the potential to manifest, and I have a lot of possibilities! I hope you can understand how powerful and exciting this is!

So, where are we now?

The boys are two years old. We've relocated from Houston to the outskirts of Nashville, Tennessee. Mom and Dad decided to go home to Gatlinburg, Tennessee, and deMarco and I felt Nashville would be a great place for us and our family. We'd always loved Tennessee and knew we'd be closer to my parents, be in music city, which couldn't hurt, and we'd have seasons again, which was really important to us. So, I sold Mom and Dad's house in Houston and our house in less than one month. Again, we made a decision, set it in motion, and the Universe supported it. It's been a big transition for all of us, but we're all adjusting, and we are so happy living in our new home. We're living in a beautiful area with beautiful rolling hills and open space. The boys have started preschool three days a week, and deMarco and I continue growing our businesses while working on our music. The school system in our county is supposedly one of the best in the country. Another example of how priorities shift when you become a parent!

Leaving for weekend gigs was too difficult for us, being separated from the boys, so we came up with an idea of going out twice per year for an extended four to five-week tour at a time, taking the boys with us. It was actually my mom's idea. She told us that she and my father would travel with us and help with the boys. So, we launched our first tour in February of 2013 and called it "Celebrating Families of Diversity." Mom and Dad joined us, and we all boarded an RV tour bus/motor home and hit the road performing over twenty concerts up the West Coast. It was an interesting experience but very rewarding. We feel this is a good model for us to use and will probably continue going out a couple times a year until the boys start school. I think it's also a powerful statement to see us, with our sons and my parents sharing our story. I trust it gives people hope, particularly young people, giving them a glimpse of what they, too, can create if they so desire in spite of what they've perhaps been told.

So, what's next? I will continue the journey, being open to the possibilities and the many lessons to come. I will be thankful for the miracle of my baby boys who are growing into little men before our eyes each day. I will be grateful for those who fulfilled their soul's contract this time around, including my amazing partner and husband who inspires me to be a better person and a better father every day. I am grateful to Lexi and her husband who loved and trusted us enough to say yes. I will treasure Mary who is forever my angel and whom I love with a heavenly love that I will never truly be able to explain. I will be forever grateful to my loving parents who have uprooted their lives to be a part of ours and who remind me of unconditional love every day. I will always remember how supportive our entire families have been through this experience. I will definitely remember those friends who came to our side, many unexpected. I have had to forgive some of those who didn't show up when we most expected.

I will never forget May 23, 2011 at 2:30 p.m. It was the day I understood "heaven on earth" and being "in this world but not of it."

And, last but not least, to my sons who remind me every day that anything is possible, *I will love you forever.*

PART II

On the Legal Side by Richard Vaughn of the IFLC

My entering the field of assisted reproduction law really was a matter of being at the right place at the right time and finding my passion. I had been working as in-house counsel for a medical device company; their priorities had changed, though, and I had left the firm. I took some time to think carefully about what I wanted to do in my career.

At the same time, my husband, Tommy, and I were serious about starting the surrogacy process. Our attorney was Will Halm, who was more than just an expert in this area of law. He and his partner were the first same-sex male couple to obtain a pre-birth order giving both of them parental rights and putting both on the birth certificate in a surrogacy case.

After talking with Will about the legal issues to be aware of, I found myself fascinated with it. That got me thinking; I was about to change my life and have a family. What better area of law could there be than to help other people who want families and to make that my entire focus.

It was like my mission statement come true: forming a family was my new personal passion, and I could make work my passion, too. I'd be working with groundbreakers.

As my partner and I were starting the surrogacy process, Will had merged his Los Angeles firm with a San Diego firm. The man who owned the San Diego firm was Will's lawyer in his surrogacy. The new firm's mission was to become a national firm in this business, and they wanted somebody who could manage it, grow it, and who was passionate about it. They named the new firm National Fertility Law Center. The idea was to take what they had been doing locally and expand nationally. There was no national firm doing this type of law at the time.

In my work with the medical device company, I had created and trained a national network of sales representatives and distributors of the products we were making, making it into a viable entity. So, when I started in fertility law, not only did I have thirteen years of experience as a lawyer, but I also had experience running a business start-up (where you wear many hats). They also wanted somebody passionate about the field of assisted reproduction and, at that time, a large part of their client base was same-sex parents, so that was another category I filled. I went through a lengthy interview process over a couple months, and it was a perfect fit.

Tommy and I signed our surrogacy agency retainer in December 2006, and our sons, Austin and Aiden, were born in August 2008.

Literally as I signed the retainer with the surrogacy agency, I was also starting this job with the NFLC. It was and is an amazing privilege. It just felt right from the beginning. There was a learning curve, of course, but once I got the basics under my belt, I felt comfortable.

We are still building a national network of attorneys. The thing about that part of the job is, it's not only learning the basics of assisted reproduction law, but learning it in all states. My job was to synthesize how we do it in California versus how it is done in other states, how treatment differs between same-sex parents versus single or married intended parents, and understanding the customs and practices in other states. Through this network, we have a unique opportunity to see how we can share best practices. In California, we are intended parent friendly; so, the question is, "Can we translate any of that to other states?" Fortunately, we have been able to do so by creating this network of attorneys who are working on cases together.

For example, one attorney in Oregon, prior to our getting involved, hadn't done much with this area of law there. The process there required that we finish the parentage application to the court *after* birth, versus in California getting the parentage order *prior* to birth. Most clients would prefer to have a prebirth order in place. Prebirth orders aren't effective until the day of birth, but you are done with the legal work; as soon as the baby comes, you are the legal parent. You can be just as legally protected in a postbirth state with the right ancillary documents in place until the court order is issued, but the perception is that prebirth is better, and in a sense it is.

The fact that California and other prebirth states allow you to go to court prior to the birth doesn't mean you have to; you can still go to court postbirth. In most states, the child's parental rights are established at the moment of birth. The baby is immediately the child of legal parents.

We've taken our experience to places where surrogacy is not common. For instance, Idaho was one of the states where we were not even sure the court would enter an order for a non-biological parent. Now, not only will the state do so, but if the parents need other relief in terms of the birth certificate, the state of Idaho will comply.

Intended parents from all over the world are coming to the United States for surrogacy in increasing numbers. In many countries, surrogacy is not legal. So, with clients coming from many countries, we have become familiar with the rules and laws that affect these clients when they go back home; we've expanded our network of attorneys from national to international. As an example of some of the nuances involved in working with international clients, if you are a single male from most Asian countries, you may need to go home with a birth certificate that has a woman's name on it because that's the only way your home country will grant citizenship to your child. These governments don't know what to do with a birth certificate that only lists one man, let alone two men. In some situations, we need to ask the court for permission to add the surrogate's name to the birth certificate, even though she is not the legal parent. Once that is done, and the child's citizenship is established in the home country, we then can request that the birth certificate in the United States be amended to remove the surrogate's name. If the parents are a same-sex couple, we can have the second father put on the amended birth certificate for their records.

Due to working internationally, eventually our two firms split, and Will and I rebranded our firm as International Fertility Law Group. In addition to our name change, the number of people from other countries who are coming to the United States for surrogacy because of the legal environment here has greatly increased. It became my job not only to understand how laws throughout the United States differ, but also how they differ from country to country all over the world in terms of how countries view surrogacy and how birth certificates are issued. Those particulars impact how the child acquires home country citizenship and how the laws deal with (or don't deal with) same-sex intended parents in these countries. As US attorneys, we can't give advice based on the law in other countries, but we do ensure our clients are aware of issues that will affect them and their child, so we have significantly increased our international network of attorneys. I research other countries' laws and speak to attorneys in the countries our clients most frequently come from, and we now have one or two go-to attorneys in each country that we can refer clients to.

This is a niche area of law, even in the United States, and even more so in other countries where surrogacy is not legal. If I don't have a referral to a family or immigration lawyer in a country that is familiar with surrogacy, I will make it my job to find one who is familiar, or find one and educate/train him or her.

When Tommy and I were going through our surrogacy, my firm did the legal work for our case, and we felt well protected.

As a lawyer, you counsel people not only on the contract but also on the nuanced aspects of the relationship between the intended parents and the surrogate. Our firm has developed its surrogacy agreements over the last twenty years of experience, so there is a very strong foundation there. Of course, the details and issues change from case to case. What you learn as a lawyer enables you to do more than just provide a contract. You actually provide counsel on items and issues that evolve out of the questions that arise from other clients during their cases. The fact that I have gone through surrogacy myself also helps me understand what the intended parents are often going through, their fears and questions.

Simply bringing some common-sense experience to the table helps keep everybody on an even keel, and it helps keep situations from becoming exaggerated. For example, if you have an overreaching intended parent who is trying to micromanage the surrogate's life, that's not going to go over very well. That wisdom comes from experience rather than from the contract. What the surrogate is eating or drinking, for example—there are certain things you can put into the contract, but you don't want to overreach. Some intended parents and attorneys want to put into the contract that the surrogate must eat organic food, use no hair dye, and so on. I ask them why they want to include those clauses: Is there a fear she won't eat healthy? If it is important to the client, is he or she willing to pay the extra cost of organic food?

I also make sure intended parents understand that, even if it's in the contract, they are not there with the surrogate 24/7, and no one will be. They still have to have a level of trust that comes from meeting with the surrogate and establishing some sort of relationship with her, addressing all the questions and issues up front and having an agency, doctor, and psychologist who carefully vet the surrogate.

As time progresses, my ability to counsel clients grows substantially, but even in the first months I had practical experience from our surrogacy to share with clients. The same is true of egg donation. Tommy and I had a failed first transfer and wondered, *Why?* Was it the surrogate? Was it the donor? I can bring that experience into the conversation with the client. You need to know a lot of science, insurance, and the legal problems involved, but there's nature also, and sometimes it doesn't work. Often, an intended parent's notion is that you've hired so many people; you're paying a lot of scientists, doctors, lawyers—so, of course it's going to work. But it doesn't always work. You have to explain to the client the risks involved. If the client's expectations are something else, he or she will be disappointed if something happens. I give the client the lay of the land before he or she goes down this road.

State laws governing surrogacy have changed a lot since I began practicing in this field six years ago. I was recently preparing a list of states where same-sex couples can both get on the birth certificate, and I compared the new list to the old version from two years ago. I was struck by the number of states where there are changes. There have been changes in the law in approximately a dozen states just between 2006 and 2012. In most states surrogacy is getting easier; in a few, it is becoming more difficult. Keeping track of those changes is just a regular part of the job.

Because this whole area of law is not governed by legislation or regulation, this leaves room for some uncertainty, but it also leaves room for creativity in planning the legal strategy and approach in any given case. Of course, no client wants to be a guinea pig of the newest creative approach, but sometimes changes in the law in the middle of a client's surrogacy require us to try a new approach. So, we regularly ask our network of attorneys about new ideas and approaches. In all states we have a Plan A, but sometimes we have to devise Plans A, B, and C.

What I've learned is this: if you find yourself up against a judge who is homophobic, or the law doesn't allow surrogacy, there are always several other ways to get things done.

For instance, when I first started with my firm, the state of Connecticut was very surrogate friendly. It allowed prebirth parental orders, and everybody was happy. But the attorney general in the state took a new position one day and wouldn't allow a nonbiological same-sex father on his child's birth certificate. The Connecticut attorney general's office instructed the state vital records office not to put two men on the birth certificate unless they received a certificate of adoption for the nonbiological father. Literally, the second parent had to go adopt his own child back home, and only then would Connecticut amend the birth certificate to add the second father.

Other states have the same requirement, but the point is Connecticut changed from surrogate friendly to not so friendly. We had several active surrogacy cases in the state at that time in which same-sex couples matched with surrogates there were suddenly not able to have both parents' names on the birth certificate. It happened to be Connecticut, a small state in a populous region, so without too much difficulty the surrogates were able to deliver in a different state where they could get a court order for both intended parents, and both were placed on the initial birth certificate. That is one example of always having a Plan B in mind.

In a North Carolina case involving a single parent from another country that needed the surrogate's name on the birth certificate, we had a judge that would grant the order, but the state attorney general told vital records not to honor the court order. In the face of such blatant defiance of a court order, we had to look for creative ways to solve the problem. The strategy we decided to use in that case also ended up happening by default because the birth came early. In every state, if a single woman is pregnant and gives birth, she can decide who to list as the father on the birth certificate as long as he is willing to sign an affidavit of paternity. That strategy can also be used in any surrogacy case, but then the surrogate is a legal parent until her name is taken off the birth certificate by virtue of a court order. The first version of the birth certificate served the intended father's need for a woman's name on the birth certificate. Subsequent to that, we petitioned the court to terminate the surrogate's presumed parental rights. The legal presumption everywhere is that the woman is the mother; you have to go into court in all surrogacy cases to rebut that presumption.

North Carolina recently passed a constitutional amendment saying only a man and woman can be married. The state also tried to pass a personhood amendment making an embryo legally a person. If the amendment had passed, IVF doctors could be accused of murder for discarding an embryo.

The personhood movement is affecting judges' opinions. There is a concern in North Carolina that any nonbiological parent, gay or straight, may have to do a second-parent adoption, which would make it more difficult for intended parents to secure their parental rights. The same thing has occurred in Tennessee, which used to have a very simple parentage process for surrogacy cases. Now, nonbiological intended parents must adopt their own child, even though, absent the parents' intent, the child would not exist.

Colorado used to be a prebirth state, but the state passed a law allowing same-sex adoption. Once the law went into effect, judges said as a result they can no longer order a prebirth order for parentage for two same-sex parents; only the biological parent is allowed to be listed on the birth certificate (and the nonbiological parent must return home for a second-parent adoption before he or she can be added to the birth certificate).

We have to stay on top of these changes because it is an evolving area of law. That is one reason it is crucial to consult with a lawyer when getting started on surrogacy and not to rely on any information on the Internet, which could easily be outdated, even if it was written two months ago.

I must also counsel with surrogacy agencies—making sure they are aware of the laws that are changing and encouraging them to seek counsel before the match is made. For example, if the intended parents' country has laws requiring a woman's name on the birth certificate, those clients can only work in a few states, and we need to know that before the surrogate match is made. The match is made based on the expressed desires of the surrogate and parents, compatible with the desires of all parties, but also needs to be based on where the law is going to allow parents to get the court order and birth certificate they need.

There have been some attempts within the legal field to create model surrogacy legislation, which works in two ways. First, the American Bar Association (ABA) ART committee of the Family Law section, in which I'm very active, has a Model Act approved by the ABA addressing surrogacy. We are now working on amendments to the Model Act to add and revise provisions to update it in accordance with the developing best practices in the field and serve as a potential model for states desiring to enact their own legislation.

There is also the Uniform Parentage Act approved in 2002 and adopted by nine states; it can also serve as a model for states to enact their own legislation.

The area of law is not one that is left to the federal government; rather, it is left to the states. But what will help create uniformity is helping people understand that it is in the best interest of the children resulting from intended reproduction to be the legal children of their intended parents from the moment of birth.

Another area I see changing is the issue of full faith and credit, in adoptions as well as surrogacy. Under the concept of full faith and credit, an order of parentage from a court in one state would be honored in another state. While there are solid constitutional grounds behind this concept, there is no uniform position on this in terms of whether surrogacy parentage orders will be recognized from state to state. In fact, only recently was Florida told by the federal appeals courts that it had to give full faith and credit to same-sex adoption orders its same-sex resident parents had obtained in other states, so it will probably be the subject of litigation in the next few years.

A lot of people see assisted reproduction technology as creating ethical questions because of what we can do with technology. I think that's always going to be the case. We'll probably see more cases pushing the envelope in terms of whether certain technical possibilities should or should not be allowed. Medical technology will always outpace the law, especially in this area. That's why it's critical to always get a consultation with a lawyer if you're utilizing any sort of assisted reproductive technology.

PART III

The Process – A Basic Outline

One thing that would have been extremely helpful for me would have been an outline, or listing in order, the processes during the journey of surrogacy. The following is a basic order of the process from start to finish when taking the journey of surrogacy. Obviously, every case is different, but our attorney helped me put this together.

1.   Find and choose a doctor and/or IVF clinic that is willing to work with you. (Believe it or not, many clinics won't).

2.   Find and choose a donor. Use a donor agency, or find a donor independently.

3.   Find and choose a surrogate. Use a surrogacy agency, or find a surrogate independently.

4.   Receive medical clearance for your donor. This can be done through the donor agency if using an agency. If you are using an independent donor, your clinic can do the clearance. In most cases, this involves a physical examination as well as a psychological evaluation.

5.   Once clearance is received, your attorney will create the egg donor contract.

6.   Receive medical clearance for the surrogate. Again, if you are using an agency, they will more than likely do the clearance. If you have an independent surrogate, your clinic will do the clearance. In most cases, this involves a physical examination as well as a psychological evaluation.

7.   Your attorney will create the surrogacy contract once clearance is given (whether this contract is first or second can vary depending on whether you find the donor or surrogate first, or if she is a traditional surrogate, being the donor and the surrogate).

8.   Create a trust account with a private escrow company, attorney or, in some limited circumstances, the surrogacy agency. This account is used to pay the surrogate and any negotiated expenses to the surrogate throughout the surrogacy. If you are using an independent surrogate, you may not have any fees (if the surrogate is doing it for free), or you may agree to pay any expenses or fees to the surrogate directly, particularly if the surrogate is

someone personally known to the intended parent(s). Regardless, the financial agreement and distribution of funds should be clearly written out in the surrogacy contract.

9. Guardianship documents are not required but ideally should be done simultaneously with the surrogacy contract. This document explains what is to happen with the embryo/fetus while in utero if something were to happen to the intended parent(s) during the surrogacy. Because the baby hasn't actually been born yet, this document protects the intended parent(s) wishes for the baby in utero, considering the parent(s) doesn't have parental rights officially until the baby is born.

10. Your attorney creates the court documents and the court order confirming parental rights for one or both parents. The attorney goes to court (usually the intended parents do not even need to attend). Once the judge signs the order, your parental rights to the child are confirmed. Take this order to the hospital with you at the time of delivery.

11. After the birth, the hospital will have a representative meet with you to go over all the information needed for the birth certificate. Make sure you know the exact name you want your child to have at this time since the name on the birth certificate will also be used for social security. In most cases, you are given a temporary birth certificate, and the official birth certificate is mailed later. In some states, you must actually order the official birth certificate online, and there are possible fees involved.

12. If the hospital insists on listing the surrogate as the mother, you will immediately need to call your attorney, and he or she will need to take your order confirming parentage to court to have the surrogate's name removed. Note: If the surrogate is listed as the mother, it is best to wait to apply for the child's social security number. The hospitals typically apply for the child's social security number at the same time they file the birth certificate. You will need to tell them not to do so if the surrogate is listed on the birth certificate. Otherwise, the surrogate will be linked to the child through the social security number, and trying to undo this will be difficult.

If the surrogate is not listed on the birth certificate or has been removed by court order, and only the biological parent is listed, and if the birth state won't enter the court order for both same-sex parents, listing both on the birth certificate, usually the non-bio parent must complete a second or step-parent adoption. This involves having your attorney, more than likely the same one you've used for the entire process, begin the process for the second or step-parent adoption. Usually, there is no time frame for this following the birth; however, until this is complete, the second parent does not have full parental rights to the child. Once this is done, the birth certificate, in most (but not all) states will be amended to add the second parent. Additionally, the cost to adopt is currently a tax credit (the only positive I could find throughout this process!).

PART IV

OTHERS' STORIES

Tommy and Rich
written by Tommy Woelfel

As gay men, when we came out, neither Rich nor I thought becoming a parent was possible.

For the longest time, in my own journey, I didn't know I would be in a long-term, lasting relationship. Yet, here I am, married to Rich and with two kids, so a lot has changed since I first discovered who I was.

I would have to say Rich brought up the idea of becoming dads and helped me realize the reality of it. Of course, as is true in most aspects of our relationship, he's the planner and the organizer. So, it's natural he would be the one to bring up the possibility of having children and say, "Hey, if we want to do this, let's start heading in this direction," which we did.

Rich had a back-and-forth relationship with the idea of having kids. He had been previously married to a woman, and the two had thought they might have kids together when they were in their thirties. Rich came out as a gay man at age twenty-seven and figured having children would never be a possibility. However, when he moved to Los Angeles, he met gay friends who were going through the process of becoming parents, which opened his eyes to the possibilities.

Then, on his way back from a business trip in the St. Louis airport, he was walking behind a family with small children, all laden with strollers and diaper bags and suitcases, the kids holding the parents' hands. He was touched by the scene and the obvious family bond. He came home that night and asked me if I had ever thought about it.

Rich did some research and talked to some guys we knew, who recommended the Pop Luck Club, a nonprofit social and resource organization for gay dads or guys who want to become dads. We went to one of their resource fairs and started collecting information about agencies and the ART process. In fact, the agency we finally selected for surrogacy—Growing Generations—was there that day, but we interviewed other agencies along the way. But even though we had begun the research process, we ended up putting the plan on hold for four or five more years.

One reason for waiting was that, although we both agreed it was something we wanted to do, neither of us was quite ready at that time. Among other things, we wanted to do some traveling first. Finally, as the time got longer and longer, we thought, "Well, we're not getting any younger."

The other reason for waiting was finances. At the Pop Luck resource fair we attended in 2002 or 2003, the cost estimates we received were in the range of $100,000 to $120,000, which over the next few years grew to $140,000. A few things came together for us during those next few years that made us feel more secure about being financially prepared for surrogacy.

Once we decided to go ahead, we interviewed several agencies for surrogacy and egg donation. In the research phase, most people find different agencies have different strengths. Part of that is going to different agencies, meeting them, talking to them. For us it was just a gut feeling, a personal choice more than anything, to go with one agency for surrogacy and a different agency for egg donation.

Also in the interview phase, of course, it's important to interview a lawyer. We met with Will Halm, who was referred to us by one of my spin class students. As it turned out, he was a founder of Growing Generations, the agency we chose for our surrogacy. In a very short time, we got a lot of information on the whole surrogacy process and the legal aspects. We felt very comfortable after talking to Will.

In the course of meeting with Will, Rich, who had been working as in-house counsel for a medical supply company, became fascinated with the field of assisted reproduction law. Long story short, Rich and Will are now business partners with a legal practice focused exclusively on ART services, International Fertility Law Group.

We liked all that Growing Generations could offer because they are probably one of the oldest and one of the largest agencies, so all the processes they have set up pretty much cover any possible situation. There was a strong sense of comfort in that. The agency originally was formed to only do surrogacy for gay clients; that was their market. They did it very well and soon became one of the biggest agencies in the country, which opened everyone's eyes to the fact there is a huge need for services for gay and lesbian intended parents.

There was the sense that Growing Generations knew and understood us and would treat us as we wanted to be treated.

One reason we were prepared was that Growing Generations did a good job of laying it all out for us. Because the founders of the agency were participants in surrogacy themselves, they personally had experienced the confusion that can arise when agencies only provide information about one part of the process. Growing Generations took a different approach and explained to clients, "This is what you can expect in all these areas…"

Growing Generations had coordinated with our egg donation agency—A Perfect Match—on numerous occasions. Most surrogacy agencies understand that if they also offer egg donation services, it's still possible clients won't find a donor with them. We felt confident and comfortable with both agencies we used; the two together worked great for us. Going with your gut sometimes is equally as important as facts and figures on paper.

We began interviewing surrogates and egg donors at the same time but found the donor first. Once you decide on a donor, the donor agency puts the donor on hold, and then you meet up and get assigned or matched up with a surrogate, which can take up to six months. We entered a donor contract in June that year and the surrogacy contract in July.

There are a lot of factors you have to talk about up front in the meeting with the surrogate—for example, is she willing to carry multiples? If your ideal is to have twins, she should be able to have twins or more.

Once we began the surrogacy process, there were a few hitches. The first embryo transfer on September 1 didn't work. The first donor cycle produced thirteen eggs, which is lower than normal but not horrible. We fertilized eleven of thirteen with ICSI, where you directly inject sperm into the egg. Of those eleven eggs fertilized, we had three worth using.

We agreed with our doctor that the eggs would be split 50/50, with half fertilized by my sperm, half by Rich's. Of course, thirteen eggs is an odd number, and Rich deferred to me. In our minds, we were in this together, even though there is no guarantee either way. Science and technology can only take you so far. God takes over from there.

The decision of whose genetic material would be used came into play even more when it came to the viability of the embryos because it came down to three. We always said going into it, we would let the doctor tell us what he or she felt. We weren't going into it saying x many from you, x many from me, because you can't guarantee that. Once the doctor determined viability, we had three usable embryos; two were mine, and one was Rich's, including one "super embryo," which was mine.

All of the embryos were day-5 blastocysts. We had discussed wanting twins. We decided to take a chance and transfer all three. In an ideal world, we were hoping we would have twins, one from my sperm, one from his.

We did not get pregnant. None took, not even the "super" one.

No doctor has a perfect way of looking at an embryo and saying, "I know this one is going to get you pregnant." Doctors look at the shape, number of cells, and so on, but there's really no perfect way of saying this embryo is good, or this one is bad.

Despite our disappointment, I don't remember ever considering using another surrogate. There was no smoking gun to say, "This is why it failed." We really liked our surrogate, from the first interview set up by the surrogacy agency. We felt really lucky that we found someone who put us all on the same page.

We looked at the donor and considered whether something might have gone wrong there. She was young and had never done this before. We had her records from the first cycle reviewed by a doctor, but no one found anything amiss other than perhaps tweaking the meds. Her grandmother had died right before the cycle; the donor was also driving up from Los Angeles every other day for monitoring. We arranged to have her monitored locally, hoping that would reduce her stress, and it worked out; we got a better cycle the second time.

When the first cycle doesn't take, it takes thirty to forty-five days before you can try again. The second time, in mid-November, we got seventeen viable eggs—better, but not great. Thirteen eggs were fertilized. On the day of the transfer, there were only four worth using, two from each of us—a disappointingly high attrition rate but apparently not uncommon.

The doctor was not thrilled with the quality of the embryos, but they were OK. Rich and I had agreed to take the doctor's advice on how many to transfer. When you transfer multiple embryos, there is a chance you will end up with a multiple birth. The chance of all four embryos taking was really low, so we weren't too scared.

But we were in a different place this go-round. It hadn't worked the first time, and we really wanted it to work. Money also factored in: each cycle with the egg donor costs in the range of $15,000 to $20,000. If we had another failed transfer, we might not have been able to do a third. We didn't have unlimited money, so we went for it and literally put all our eggs in one basket.

We decided to transfer all four embryos. When selecting the surrogate, we had already determined she would be willing to carry multiples if need be. She wasn't looking forward to carrying a whole litter of kids inside her but, like us, she listened to the doctor. The doctor's opinion came first, and then we would discuss personal desires based on that. At that point, the surrogate knew what our hopes were; we were all on the same page on how to get there.

The transfer was right around Thanksgiving. In early December, we confirmed the pregnancy, the same day we went to a huge Christmas party with a lot of our friends. Although conventional wisdom is that it's best not to tell family and friends about a new pregnancy until after the first trimester, we were so excited that we told everyone.

It took ten days from the transfer to find out we were pregnant. The blood test measures the level of hormones in the blood; if they are elevated, you are definitely pregnant. The higher the levels of elevation, the more likely it could be multiples. The indication was it might be twins.

The pregnancy went smoothly; fortunately, we had a great surrogate. You've got those lines that sometimes get crossed, whether one is too smothering, too distant, too controlling, or not involved enough. Our surrogate was married and had two kids of her own; she had a life. On the positive side of that, she had two great kids; she was a good mother. We didn't have to worry about what kind of surrogate she was going to be—being pregnant was easy for her, and it's one of the reasons she chose to be a surrogate. Because we could see what kind of family she was raising, what kind of mother she was, we were confident.

On the other hand, we had to respect the fact she had her own family, her own kids. We didn't want to be too involved in her life, not too needy. She was very open and cooperative as far as our being involved in milestone moments throughout the pregnancy. We were there for the ultrasound, for most of the labor, and for the entire birth. She was completely fine and open and great about our being as involved as we wanted to be.

We checked in with her about every three weeks during the pregnancy. We also recorded messages to the babies and e-mailed the MP3 files to her. She downloaded the files and put headphones on her belly and played messages for the kids, something she and her husband had done when he had to be away during her earlier pregnancies.

I feel we were extremely lucky. Even though our surrogate was a first-time surrogate, she was on the same page with us from the very beginning. She was aware she was helping us create a family, and it made her happy she was able to help us do that.

There are some business aspects to the relationship with the surrogate, but our agency played a good intermediary. There was never anything awkward we had to discuss. We were matched very well and got along very well from the beginning.

We chose not to know which of us was the biological father. It didn't matter to us. We didn't even know on the day of the birth; it took a while to get a feel for what we thought. We still haven't done a DNA test. We have reasons to feel one is "his" and one is "mine," but we still don't know for sure.

Even when we were planning it, it was an ideal to have twins with one fathered by Rich, one by me. Both of us wanted our own genetic children if we could do that. But it's not like it was all about that; we would both be happy no matter the outcome. We had discussed what we would do if only one embryo took, only one child was born, including the possibility of having another. I wanted twin boys; Rich just wanted them to be healthy and happy. We did everything we could logically to allow that to happen, but we didn't do a PGD (pre-implantation genetic diagnosis) to determine DNA or gender. Fortunately, it does appear it turned out the way we had hoped.

Our boys were born August 9, 2008, and were carried to thirty-eight weeks. They were pretty big and healthy by the time they came out.

For anyone considering becoming a parent through surrogacy, once you decide this is the path for you, it's important to slow down and take time to make sure you've had all the crucial conversations. So many people, once they decide, seem to want to rush into it—before they even know all the questions to ask. Also, it's important to develop some level of trust in your surrogate and not try to micromanage the process. You have to understand that it may be your baby or babies, but it's her body, and you have to respect that.

It is important to be sure you are ready, but don't wait too long. It is impossible to be 100 percent ready; there's always going to be something else you want to get done first—make a certain amount of money or add a room onto the house…But in the big picture, you need to be willing to have your life change. That doesn't mean giving up who you are; you will be a better parent if you stay true to who you are. Plan, but don't get hung up on too many small details. Being a dad is a lot of work, but it's also a lot of fun and joy that far outweighs the sacrifices.

Looking back now, knowing what we know and spending what we spent, would we do it all over again? Yes, in a heartbeat.

But will we do it again? No. We're very comfortable with our family, very set, very dedicated to these boys. Some people are able to handle bigger families, but this is the right number for us.

We were fortunate. This is what we wanted; we got where we wanted to be. Of course, once your children are born, the journey and the joy and labor of love continues and never stops filling your life.

Case Studies by Dr. Samuel Pang

The following are the true stories of five gay male couples that Dr. Samuel Pang has helped over the past eight years. Their names have been changed to protect their confidentiality, but all of their stories are real. These cases were selected to illustrate the variety of experiences that gay couples encounter during their journey to parenthood through egg donation and gestational surrogacy and intentionally include the pitfalls and risks that they have encountered during their path to parenthood. As you will see, some were very fortunate to sail through easily, but others experienced grueling journeys. Nevertheless, the tenacity and perseverance of these couples demonstrate their determination to have a family. Their stories are truly inspirational.

Jeremy and Alexander

Shortly after they began dating in March 2002, Jeremy (42) and Alex (39) began discussing their plans to have children and sought the assistance of an egg donor and surrogacy agency. By the time they married in July 2004, they had an egg donor selected, but finding a gestational surrogate took more time. They eventually secured a gestational surrogate but, by then, their original egg donor backed out because her life situation had changed, and she was no longer in a position to be an egg donor, so they had to find a different egg donor and hope that their gestational surrogate would wait for them. Their gestational surrogate was a thirty-three-year-old married woman who had three children, and they didn't want to have any more children of their own, but she loved being pregnant.

After finding another appropriate egg donor, Jeremy and Alex proceeded with their IVF cycle in March 2005. Of the twelve eggs retrieved from their egg donor, six were inseminated with Jeremy's sperm, and the other six were inseminated with Alex's sperm. One embryo from each cohort was transferred into their gestational surrogate, resulting in a singleton pregnancy, and six embryos were frozen (three from each cohort). Halfway through the pregnancy, their gestational surrogate began bleeding at twenty weeks' gestation.

She ended up on complete bed rest for ten weeks, bleeding every single day of those ten weeks. She eventually went into labor, and their baby boy was delivered by Cesarean section in October 2005, ten weeks prematurely. He spent eleven weeks in the Neonatal Intensive Care Unit before being able to go home, but despite his rough beginnings, he is now a healthy boy.

Paternity testing confirmed that he was the genetic child of Alex, so their plan was to attempt another pregnancy using frozen embryos created from Jeremy's sperm. Not wishing to risk a twin pregnancy (which is more likely to result in premature birth), they elected to transfer only one frozen embryo into a different gestational surrogate in September 2006. This resulted in an identical twin pregnancy which miscarried at twelve weeks, the week before Christmas 2006. They were disappointed but, at the same time, relieved.

The miscarriage was a traumatic experience for their gestational surrogate, who decided not to try again, so the agency had to find a different gestational surrogate for Jeremy and Alex. They were eventually matched to another gestational surrogate, but just as they were getting ready to proceed with another frozen embryo transfer in April 2007, she became pregnant accidentally with her husband, so the match had to be dissolved. The agency matched them to yet another gestational surrogate, and they proceeded with their second frozen embryo transfer in October 2007. A single frozen embryo was thawed and transferred, resulting in pregnancy but an early miscarriage at six weeks. The gestational surrogate decided not to try again as her life situation had changed, and she was moving out of state, so the agency had to search for yet another gestational surrogate for Jeremy and Alex.

They were eventually matched to another gestational surrogate, which was now the fifth gestational surrogate with whom they had been matched. She was a thirty-two-year-old married woman who had two children of her own, and who had been a gestational surrogate successfully twice before, for a heterosexual couple. They went on to attempt another frozen embryo transfer in June 2008, but the third frozen embryo (created from Jeremy's sperm) did not survive the thaw, so the embryo transfer procedure was canceled.

Having used up the three frozen embryos, which had been created from Jeremy's sperm, they sought the assistance of the agency to inquire if their original egg donor would consider donating eggs to them a second time. Thankfully, she agreed to do so, and she proceeded to do a second egg donor cycle in September 2008. This time, all twelve eggs retrieved were inseminated with Jeremy's sperm, and a single embryo was transferred into their gestational surrogate, resulting in a successful pregnancy. Jeremy and Alex welcomed their second son who was born in July 2009. They now consider their family complete, with two sons who are genetic half siblings from the same egg donor, but one from Alex's sperm and the other from Jeremy's sperm.

Charles and Jonathan

Chuck and Jon were both thirty-seven years old when they came to see me in August 2005. They had married the previous year when Massachusetts became the first state in the United States to allow same-sex couples to marry. Chuck is a physician at one of the large Harvard Medical School teaching hospitals, so he approached the IVF program at that hospital, seeking their assistance to have a baby via egg donation and gestational surrogacy. That IVF program had never before treated a gay male couple, so Chuck and Jon were told their request would need to be presented to the hospital ethics committee for consideration. Chuck and Jon were offended that their request for assistance to have a baby could be construed as "unethical" and needed to be "cleared" by an ethics committee. They came to see me for a consultation after they discovered that I had welcomed treating gay male couples since 1998.

Chuck's sister was forty years old and had agreed to be their gestational surrogate. Jon's sister was thirty-five years old and had agreed to be their egg donor. They proceeded to do an IVF cycle in October 2005, with Jon's sister donating her eggs, inseminated with sperm provided by Chuck. They wanted only one child and did not want to risk twins, so they chose to transfer a single embryo into the uterus of Chuck's sister, their gestational surrogate. This resulted in a successful pregnancy, and she delivered a healthy baby boy in July 2006.

Jerry and Frank

Jerry (33) and Frank (31) came to see me in August 2007. They had been in a relationship for two years and wanted to have a baby through egg donation and gestational surrogacy. They needed to find an egg donor and a gestational surrogate through an agency.

After they were successfully matched with an egg donor and a gestational surrogate, they proceeded to do their IVF treatment in November 2007. Of the sixteen eggs retrieved from their egg donor, eight were inseminated with Jerry's sperm, and the other eight were inseminated with Frank's sperm. One embryo from each cohort was transferred into the uterus of their gestational surrogate, and she conceived successfully, delivering a healthy baby girl in July 2008. Through paternity testing, it was determined that she was Jerry's genetic child.

From their original IVF treatment, eight embryos had been frozen, three embryos from Jerry's sperm and five embryos from Frank's sperm. They returned in November 2009 to attempt another pregnancy with the same gestational surrogate. Two of the five frozen embryos, which had been created with Frank's sperm, were thawed and transferred into the uterus of their gestational surrogate. She conceived successfully again and went on to deliver another healthy baby girl in August 2010. They now have two daughters who are genetic half siblings through the same egg donor, one being Jerry's genetic child and the other being Frank's genetic child.

Gavin and Keith

Gavin (31) and Keith (45) had been together for five years when they came to me in November 2008. They had selected an egg donor and a gestational surrogate through an agency. Their gestational surrogate was a twenty-five-year-old married woman who had two children, both delivered by Cesarean section, and she had no plans to have more children of their own.

Shortly after their consultation with me, their original egg donor backed out, so they needed to select a different egg donor. They eventually proceeded with their IVF process in June 2009. They decided that only Gavin would be the "bio dad," so all fifteen eggs retrieved from their egg donor were inseminated with Gavin's sperm. Two (2) embryos were transferred into their gestational surrogate, resulting in a successful singleton pregnancy. However, because of her two prior Cesarean-section births, the placenta invaded deep into the muscle of her uterus at the site of the previous Cesarean section scar, resulting in a complication known as *placenta accreta*. Their healthy baby girl was delivered in March 2010 by Cesarean section, but their surrogate needed to have a hysterectomy immediately following the birth. Although this is an extremely rare complication of pregnancy, this event was a sober reminder that pregnancy, per se, carries some risks.

Oscar and Kenneth

Oscar (43) and Ken (42) had already selected an egg donor and gestational surrogate through an agency when they came to see me in September 2010. Although they had been in a relationship for eight years, they had recently married in June 2010. During the course of the evaluation of their first egg donor, she was determined to be medically unsuitable to be an egg donor, and so they had to select a different egg donor. They eventually selected another egg donor and proceeded with their IVF treatment in February 2011. Twenty-nine eggs were retrieved from their egg donor; fourteen were inseminated with Oscar's sperm, and fifteen were inseminated with Ken's sperm. All twenty-nine of the eggs fertilized, but despite the large number of fertilized eggs, the embryo development was mostly poor, such that only eight embryos were usable. Two embryos (one from each cohort) were transferred into their gestational surrogate, and the remaining six embryos were frozen (three from each cohort). Unfortunately, pregnancy did not ensue.

They returned for a frozen embryo transfer in April 2011, with the intention of transferring one thawed embryo from each cohort. Only one of three frozen embryos from Oscar's cohort survived the thaw, and one of two frozen embryos from Ken's cohort survived the thaw. Unfortunately, neither of the two embryos implanted following transfer into their gestational surrogate, and pregnancy did not result. They were left with only one remaining frozen embryo.

At this point, they decided to attempt another IVF cycle using a different egg donor. They proceeded with their second IVF cycle in December 2011, with fifteen eggs retrieved from this egg donor. This time, eight eggs were inseminated with Oscar's sperm, and seven were inseminated with Ken's sperm. To our surprise, only one of the fifteen eggs fertilized, but it did not proceed to develop into an embryo, and so there was no embryo transfer. In our efforts to investigate the reason that fertilization did not happen, we confirmed that fertilization resulted normally in all the other IVF cases that same day. Given that all the cases that day shared the same batch of embryo culture media and incubator, we deduced that the failure of fertilization was likely associated with a previously undiagnosed egg factor.

Over 95 percent of the male couples that I have treated have achieved pregnancy with either their first or second attempt, so this was a highly unusual situation. Needless to say, Oscar and Ken were devastated by their bad luck. They had spent many thousands of dollars paying for two different egg donors and had not yet achieved pregnancy. They needed to save up more money before they could afford to attempt a third IVF treatment.

Meanwhile, new technology was emerging that would ultimately help Oscar and Ken achieve their pregnancy. For decades, while embryo freezing has been relatively successful since the early 1980s, egg freezing had been extremely challenging because only about 1 percent of frozen eggs would survive the thaw. However, a new method of egg freezing called vitrification emerged several years ago and was discovered to work extremely well for freezing eggs. An IVF program in Atlanta has been vitrifying donor eggs experimentally since 2006, achieving an average live birth rate of 60 percent using frozen donor eggs, and they have reported over five hundred live births from frozen donor eggs since 2007.

I offered Oscar and Ken the option of using frozen donor eggs from this frozen donor egg bank, at a significantly lower cost than using fresh donor eggs from another egg donor matched through the egg donor agency. After extensive counseling, they agreed to use frozen donor eggs for their third

IVF treatment. They selected an egg donor from the list of available donors at the frozen donor egg bank website, and eight frozen eggs were shipped from Atlanta to Boston in July 2012. All eight of the frozen donor eggs survived the thaw; four were inseminated with Oscar's sperm, and four were inseminated with Ken's sperm. One embryo from each cohort was transferred into their gestational surrogate, and she gave birth to twins in April 2013.

In October 2012, the American Society for Reproductive Medicine (ASRM) officially declared that egg freezing is no longer considered "experimental." Therefore, going forward, in addition to the use of known egg donors (family members or a close friend) or anonymous/recruited egg donors (through an egg donor agency), there is now also the third option to use frozen donor eggs from a donor egg bank.

CPSIA information can be obtained
at www.ICGtesting.com
Printed in the USA
LVHW080337230321
682200LV00014B/432